Worlds of
ENGLISH
and
DRAMA
Giles Bird and Jay Norris

Illustrated by
Robert Salmon and Martin White

Oxford University Press 1983

Oxford University Press, Walton Street, Oxford OX2 6DP

Oxford   London   Glasgow
New York   Toronto   Melbourne   Auckland
Kuala Lumpur   Singapore   Hong Kong   Tokyo
Delhi   Bombay   Calcutta   Madras   Karachi
Nairobi   Dar es Salaam   Cape Town

and associated companies in
Beirut   Berlin   Ibadan   Mexico City   Nicosia

Oxford is a trade mark of Oxford University Press

© Oxford University Press 1983

ISBN 0 19 833163 0

Teachers may reproduce the quizword
pages for classroom use without obtaining
permission from the publisher.

Typeset in Great Britain by
Rowland Phototypesetting, Bury St Edmunds
and printed by William Clowes (Beccles) Ltd.

Contents

Introduction   4

1   The world of responsibility
      The Making of the Earth   Nigeria   7

2   The world of trickery
      The Apples of Iduna   Scandinavia   19

3   The world of cruelty
      The Day the Creek went Dry   Australia (Aborigine)   31

4   The world of mysteries
      The Seven Black Stones   France   43

5   The world of darkness
      The Dead Moon   England   55

6   The world of rivalry
      The Final Victory   Canada (Inuit)   67

7   The world of surprises
      The Man of Many Mistakes   India   79

8   The world of courage
      The Journey to the Sun   American Indian   91

9   The world of despair
      The Two Brothers   Soviet Union   103

10   The world of wisdom
       The Gift of the Gods   Mexico (Aztec)   115

Index   127

Introduction

Worlds of English and Drama is constructed around ten little-known myths and legends. The stories come from a variety of cultures, but they are all concerned with people: their problems and their relationships. The ideas, around which these tales have grown, are universal and timeless.

These stories possess a unity that extracts from contemporary fiction are unable to match, and they are unrivalled in the richness of their themes. The contribution that myths and legends may make towards children's understanding of the similarity and kinship of peoples, whatever their culture or era, should never be underestimated.

Every chapter forms a recognizable sequence of units:

The story
Question box
Exploring ideas
Discovering words
Quizword
Who's in it? What happens?
Step in to the drama world

The story is told in a direct, uncomplicated style, which deliberately avoids dialogue and detailed descriptions, so that no subsequent activity should be derivative or constrained.

Question box presents ten questions in two groups: the first five ensure understanding of the story-line; the second set broaden the scope of discussion and involve inferential answers.

Exploring ideas contains six activities that stem from the story. They cover both divergent and convergent situations and can be attempted orally or in writing. Obviously, there are more ideas than any class or individual child could follow up. We have deliberately offered a good choice of topics.

Discovering words is composed of three out of five areas of language use related to some incident or facet of the story. The headings and symbols identify the skill that is practised:

Learn the language: identification of major parts of speech. Nouns, adjectives, verbs, adverbs, and conjunctions are each introduced twice in the course of the book.

Make a stop: skills of punctuation

Watch your step: choosing the right word for the right place

Try a new way: using words in an unfamiliar or enterprising way

Read the signs: sorting out a puzzling meaning

Quizword is a simple crossword constructed inside a shape associated with the story, which offers an accuracy test within the challenge of a puzzle.

Who's in it? What happens? comprises an outline of characters and events. This may be studied as a quick synopsis of the gist of the story, or as an example exercise in elementary summary. In addition, this page can be treated as an instant cast-list and skeletal scenario for any direct dramatic interpretation of the tale.

Step into the drama world provides four stages for involvement in educational drama. The themes relate to the present day as well as to the original narrative and this link is clarified by the 'STEPS' at the start of the section. Each activity is carefully planned and explained by precise instructions so that the outcome should be satisfying for both pupils and teachers who are not necessarily expert in drama. The drama unit that concludes each chapter presents a superb opportunity for the vital development of children's understanding of themselves and others, through areas of experience that complement classroom work in English.

We hope that the substantial choice of follow-up pursuits will be appreciated by children in terms of variety of interest, and by teachers in terms of the structure of activities and skills which should support their educational goals. The appeal of these ancient myths and legends is still considerable and we believe that their magic will be enjoyed equally by pupils and teachers.

Jay Norris   Giles Bird

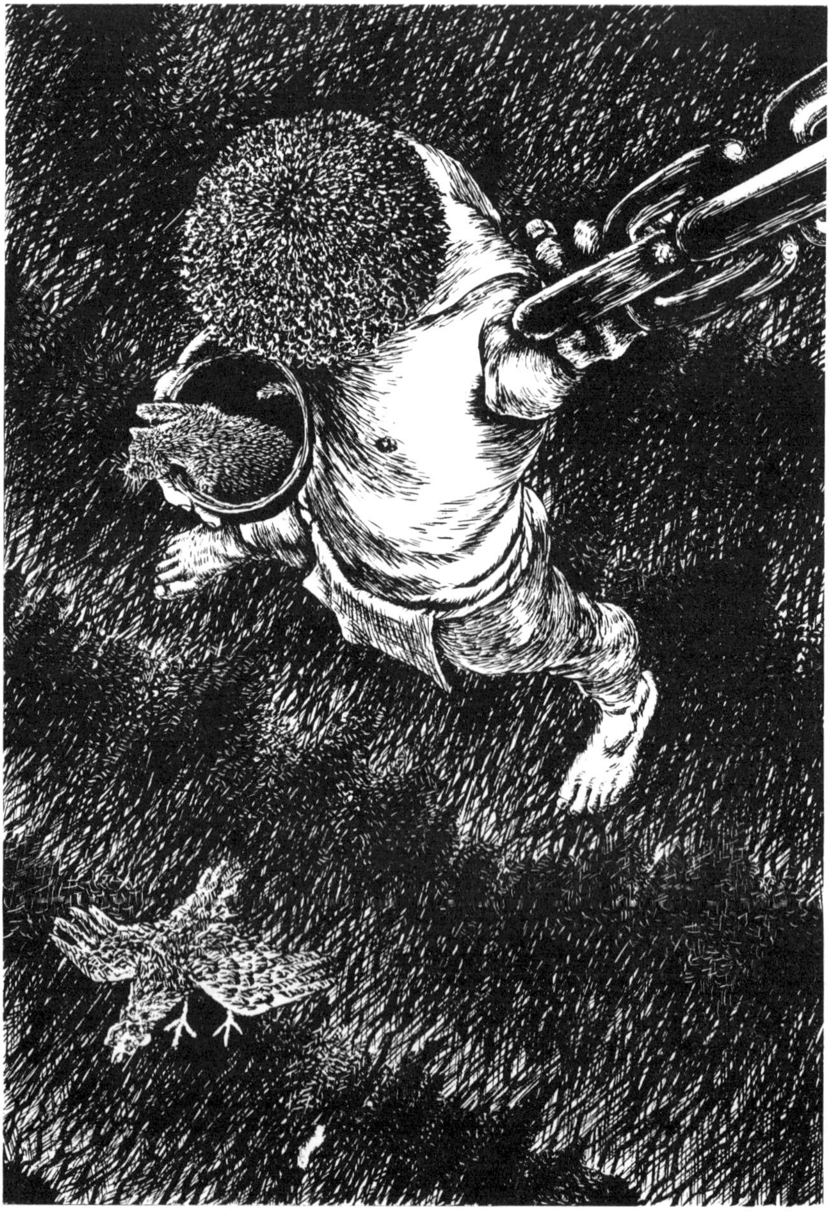

1 The world of responsibility

The Making of the Earth

Before the Earth was made, the gods lived in the sky ruled by their king, Olorun. Below the sky there was only water and black, swirling mist. One of the gods, Obatala, gained permission from Olorun to try to make land there.

Olorun told him to go for advice to Orunmila, the goddess who could foresee the future by throwing palm nuts onto a tray and studying the patterns they made. She told him that he would need a golden chain to reach down to the waters below, a snail-shell full of sand, a hen, a palm-nut and a cat.

So Obatala went to the goldsmith and asked him to make the chain. The goldsmith set to work, but he found that there was not enough gold in the sky to make a chain that would be long enough to reach the waters. In despair, Obatala asked all the gods and goddesses to give their golden jewellery to be melted down, but still the chain was too short. However, he was determined to make the journey.

One end of the long chain was fixed to the edge of the sky with a golden hook, and the other end hung down into the darkness. Orunmila brought the snail-shell full of sand, the hen, the palm-nut and the cat, and Obatala started to climb down.

Soon the black mists surrounded him and he was afraid, but down and down he climbed until, suddenly, he reached the end of the chain. He could hear the roar of the waters far below and he began to tremble. Just as he felt that he would fall and be drowned, he heard the voice of Orunmila cry, 'The sand!'. So he poured the sand out of the shell. Then the voice said, 'The hen!', and he dropped the hen, which fluttered down and started to scratch the sand over the waters. The sand fell unevenly, making mountains and valleys, and Obatala let go of the chain and fell safely onto dry land with the cat.

Here he planted the palm-nut, and at once a tree sprang up, ripened, and dropped more palm-nuts so that many trees grew. He built a hut and lived in it with his cat.

In the sky, Olorun wondered how the making of land was progressing, so he sent a messenger to find out. Obatala asked him to beg Olorun for warmth and light as the earth was so cold and dark. When the king of the gods heard the request, he made the sun and set it on its journey in the heavens.

As time passed, Obatala grew lonely and decided to create people to keep him company. He made clay into shapes of men and women and put them in the sun to dry. The work was hard and he grew very tired and thirsty, so he took sap from the palm trees and made it into wine.

When he had had a long drink, he felt much better and made many more shapes. The wine, however, had made his fingers clumsy and some of the figures had deformed arms and legs, or crooked backs, while some had no eyes.

After he had finished, Obatala looked around and was pleased with all that he had done, so he prayed to Olorun to bring the clay figures to life. The king of the gods heard his prayer, leant over the edge of the sky, and breathed the breath of life. At once the men and women rose from the sand and began to work. They chopped down trees and started to build a city.

It was then that Obatala saw that many of them were lame or blind and he realized that, because of the wine, he had made many mistakes. He was very ashamed of the suffering he had caused, so he made a vow never to drink wine again and to be the protector of all crippled people.

The men and women completed the city and made Obatala their king. He ruled them well, caring for them as a father cares for his children.

Question box

What was there before the earth was made?
What happened to the sand after the hen scratched it?
Why was the cat important to Obatala?
What was used to make the shapes of men and women?
What was the vow that Obatala made?

Do the other gods help Obatala in any way?
Where does Obatala show he is brave?
Why were the palm-nuts useful?
Do you think that Obatala would have made a good king?
How important is Olorun in the making of the Earth?

Exploring ideas

1 Fair's fair

Imagine that you are Obatala, responsible for all the people. Already you have made some mistakes, and you can see how easy it is for things to go wrong.

To make life fair and happy for everyone, you wish to give your people **five good laws**. These should be especially suited to the world that you, Obatala, have created.

Choose what you think are five important rules which would make this world a happy one. Write them down, together with your reasons for choosing each of them.

2 Just a touch

If you close your eyes and touch something, you can get a 'picture' of it through your fingertips. You can learn a lot about its shape, surface, warmth and movement this way.

In the story, Obatala has to rely on his sense of touch, because he lives in the dark until Olorun puts the sun in the sky.

a) Try and describe the feel of the hen or the cat or a palm tree.
b) Now, in the same way, describe some other things that you could find in *your* world.

3 A world of your own

A MYTH is a story which sets out to explain something for which there is no certain explanation. 'The Making of the Earth' is how the Yoruba people of West Africa have explained the Creation. How the Earth was made is told in a different way in the Book of Genesis in the Bible.

Imagine that an Eskimo, long ago, wanted to give an explanation of the Creation to his child. Frozen earth, snow and ice, seals and polar bears would all play a part in his story. Begin: 'Once upon a time . . .'

4 Invent-a-god

People have often believed that 'super-beings' or 'gods' cause all the sorrows and joys of life. These gods may look like human-beings, but they are much more powerful. To those who believe in them, they appear to control at least some of the important things of life.

Imagine that we wanted to explain our modern 'miracles' like telephones, aeroplanes, televisions, parking-meters, and other machines by inventing suitable 'gods'. These 'super-beings' will each need a special name, a definite personality, and an impressive appearance. Think how they could have given their 'gifts' to mankind.

Invent your 'gods' and 'goddesses'. Explain how they affect people's lives.

5   Just good friends

To a lot of people an animal, like Obatala's cat, is a very important part of their lives. Sometimes it is just for company, sometimes for love, and sometimes the animal helps its owner in a practical way.

Newspapers and magazines love stories about animals. Here are five headlines where animals must have done something special:

Choose one of these headlines, and write the report that you think might have followed it. You could set it out like front-page news, drawing a 'photograph' to go with it.

BOW-WOW WAS A WOW

HORSE-SENSE

A GOLDFISH IN A MILLION

CALAMITY CAT

BUDGIE SAVES THE DAY

6   Shame on you

We have all been 'ashamed of ourselves' at one time or another. We may have done something which has turned out unhappily, or perhaps we have felt that we have looked foolish.

Feelings that are as strong and as sharp as this, are often best expressed by writing a poem.
Doing it this way should help you:

- **First:** Write out any ideas for your poem in rough. You will need to make changes as you think about it.
- **Second:** Choose your words carefully to give a vivid picture of what happened. This is more important than trying to make words rhyme.
- **Third:** Make your poem honest and personal. Try to remember what went through your mind and the details of feeling personally uncomfortable.

Discovering words

Make a stop

When Obatala gave a note to the messenger, it must have been written in the dark.

> please help me olorun it is so cold down here orunmila never told me i would need a thick coat i cannot see anything you would not believe how miserable i am yesterday i could not find the door to let my dear cat in in all truth this is awful what i need is some heat to warm us up quickly help me soon olorun please i am so very unhappy how i long for the good old days in the sky on earth there is nothing i can look forward to you alone can save me good bye for now

Decide where the sentences begin and end. Rewrite the message in straight lines with full stops and capital letters in the right places.

Learn the language

Everything has a name. It might be the name of a **person**, such as Obatala, or an **animal** like 'cat', or a **place** like 'city', or a **thing** like 'wine', or even a **feeling** or an **idea** like 'despair' and 'advice'.

a) In the first paragraph of the story there are ten different **name words**. Try and discover them, then list them.
b) The sentences below make no sense at all because the **name words** have been switched around. Put them right.
1 The hen had made his wine clumsy.
2 Orunmila went to the palm-nut and asked him to make the city.
3 Below the cat there was only chain and black, swirling sand.
4 Obatala brought the goldsmith full of mist, the sky, the fingers and the trees.
5 They chopped down water and started to build a snail-shell.

Read the signs

If somebody can 'foresee the future', they may try to make their ideas sound exciting and mysterious. Here is a speech which appears to predict future events:

'As I peer through the veiled curtain of time, the dark mists clear and your future lies before me.
I see you, with the passing of the years, resident in the greatest metropolis in our land. You have been placed there by the will of many people after a victory over others who opposed you. A decade will be spent as the representative of others in an ancient edifice, surmounted by a famous clock, near a great river. Your heart will become entwined with another's, one skilled in the art of healing. A gold band will join you to this person. Your progeny shall number as the fingers of one hand: strangely, a pair of pairs, yet each pair composed of opposite genders. You yearn to know the world beneath distant skies, and, when time allows, you will pass above the water to the Land of the Rising Sun, and on to the New World. There you will reside until . . . but now the mists return. I may see no more!'

Use your dictionary, and your imagination, to help you try and sort this out. Write the predictions down in clear, simple statements.

The golden chain of Obatala quizword

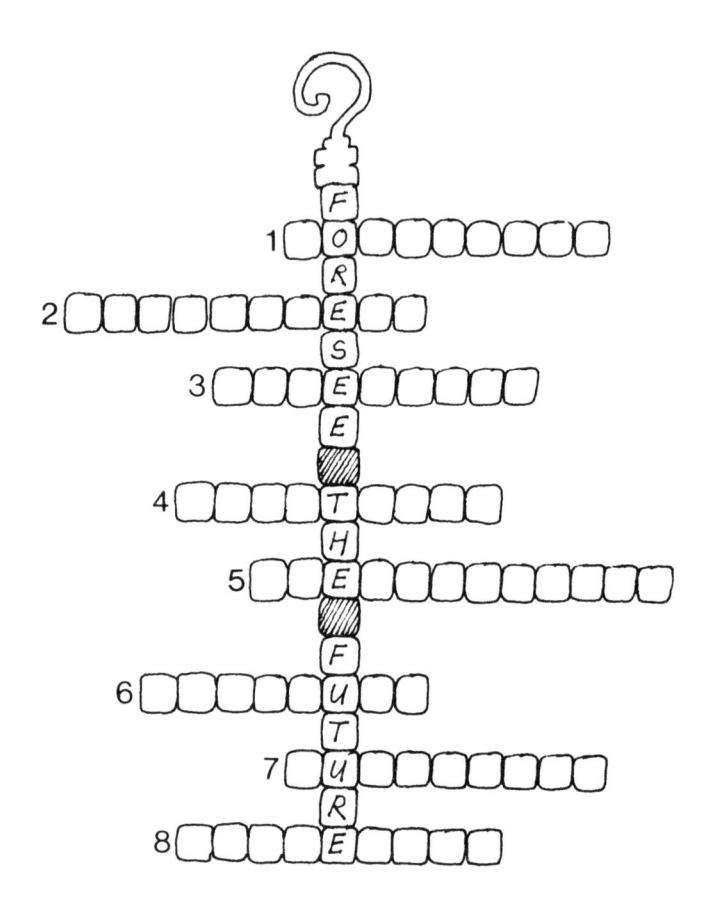

Find the words from the story.

1. Obatala went to the ___ and asked him to make the chain.
2. a ___ full of sand (2 words)
3. Obatala asked all the gods and goddesses to give their golden ___
4. The sand fell unevenly making ___ and valleys.
5. The king of the gods heard his prayer and breathed the ___ (3 words)
6. a tree sprang up, ripened, and dropped more ___ (2 words)
7. He was very ashamed of all the ___ he had caused.
8. he made a vow to be the ___ of all crippled people.

The world of Obatala

This story of creation comes from the Yoruba people of Nigeria in West Africa. The gods in these stories have to deal with human problems. These gods may be based on people who once lived and ruled cities in Nigeria long ago.

Who's in it?

Olorun...(Ol-or-un) ....the king of the gods
Obatala...(Ober-tar-ler)..........the god who makes the Earth
Orunmila...(Or-un-mill-er).......the goddess who foretells the future

The goldsmith	The messenger
The cat	Other gods and goddesses
The hen	Humans made from clay

What happens?

1. Obatala asks Olorun for permission to make land among the waters.
2. Orunmila gives advice to Obatala.
3. The goldsmith is asked to make a golden chain, and other gods are persuaded to give up their gold jewellery.
4. Obatala climbs down the chain and leaps into the darkness.
5. He plants palm-nuts that grow into trees, and builds himself a hut.
6. Because Obatala asks the messenger for heat and light, Olorun puts the sun in the sky.
7. Obatala is lonely, so he decides to create people from clay.
8. He drinks too much wine and shapes the clay carelessly.
9. After Olorun has breathed life into the clay, Obatala is ashamed to see that some of the humans are handicapped.
10. The people build a city and make Obatala their king.

Step into the drama world

Obatala comes down to make the Earth, but he also makes mistakes that he regrets.

Step one   He has enough trust to fall into the darkness.
Step two   He chooses to take on new responsibility.
Step three   Other lives suffer because he drinks too much.
Step four   He succeeds in making up for his mistakes.

      And it can happen now . . . . .

Step one

Find a partner A and B

Decide which of you is A, and which of you is B. A stands a pace behind B, checking that he is the right distance by resting his hands on B's shoulders. B must stand up straight, feet together, arms slightly out from his body. A is going to catch B by sliding his arms under B's, when B falls backwards. B closes his eyes, and when A says 'READY', will let himself fall backwards. B must trust A, and not try to 'save himself' by moving his feet. A is responsible for catching B safely. Change places after you have done this successfully several times.

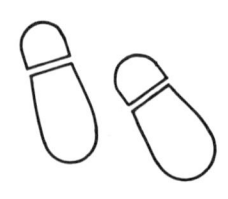

Step two

Find a partner A and B

A owns an animal, but needs to go away for a few days. His friend B, knowing this, offers to look after the pet for him. A is very worried that B may not be able to manage, so he makes very clear all the difficulties involved in looking after this pet. B is very keen to take on the responsibility. He has good answers to all the problems that A is anxious about. How does B persuade A to trust him?

Step three

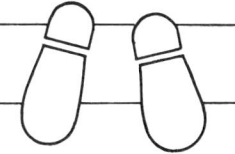

Groups of three A, B and C

A got drunk at a party and caused a car crash. A was unhurt, but B and C were injured. They are now recovering in hospital in the same ward. A visits them, wanting to apologize. He is prepared for their anger because he knows he is guilty.
To his amazement and embarrassment, they do not try to blame him at all.
The guilt that A can not escape leads him to the final words: 'I will *never* drink again!'

                        Act it out.

Step four

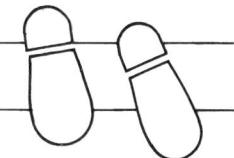

Groups of four or five

One of the group is going to be X. Everyone is going to come to a lift and enter it. After the doors are shut, X presses the buttons to reach the right floors. By mistake he also presses another button labelled 'EMERGENCY STOP'. This brings the lift to a sudden halt *between* floors. The lift is sound-proofed, so shouting is useless. X takes on the responsibility of calming down, or cheering up, the others in the lift. By the time that rescue arrives, everyone has confidence in X. His original mistake has been forgotten.

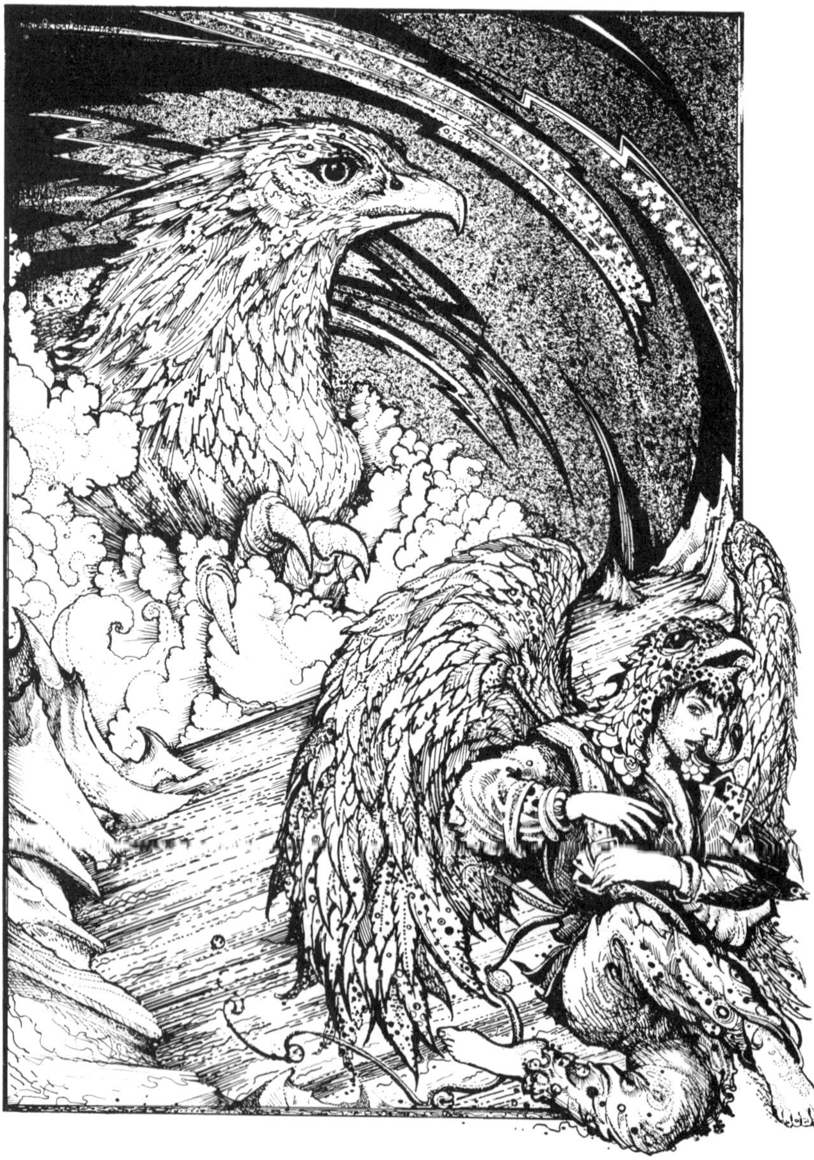

2 The world of trickery

The Apples of Iduna

In the lands of the north, the people lived among frozen mountains and gloomy forests. Only the gods enjoyed a life of complete happiness. High up in their palace at Asgard, they were surrounded by splendour and sunshine.

One of the gods, Bragi, was married to Iduna, the beautiful goddess of youth. She always carried a golden casket, full of apples from the Tree of Life. These apples warded off ill health and old age, and, whenever Iduna opened the golden casket to give fruit to the gods, she found it full.

The storm giant, Thiassi, who lived in a cold cave on earth, longed to possess the apples of youth. He did not dare to enter the palace of Asgard but one day he managed to capture Loki, the mischief-making god. To gain his freedom, Loki promised the giant that he would help to trap Iduna and her golden casket.

So Loki found Iduna in the palace of the gods and persuaded her that he knew of an orchard beyond the city walls, where there grew apples more magnificent than any in her casket. Iduna believed Loki's clever lies and agreed to go with him to see this remarkable fruit. As soon as they were outside the safety of Asgard, the sky turned dark above them. When Iduna looked up, she saw a huge eagle with outstretched claws about to swoop upon her. It was Thiassi, the storm giant, in disguise. Seizing the terrified goddess and her precious casket, he carried her far away to his cave in the land of the giants.

The Palace of Asgard now seemed silent and sad without Iduna and the apples of youth. The gods began to suffer from the tiredness of old age and their world became cold and grey.

Many days passed before Bragi was able to discover that it was Loki who had betrayed Iduna. The gods were angry and their threats frightened Loki so much that he begged to be given the chance to rescue the goddess. So he disguised himself in the shape of a falcon and flew off to the land of the giants.

After a long search, Loki found Iduna alone in a freezing cave. She had refused to give Thiassi any of the apples of youth from her golden casket and this prison was her punishment. Loki used his magic powers to change her into a swallow and her casket into a hazel nut. Then he clutched her firmly in his falcon claws and set out to fly back to Asgard. But Thiassi saw them escaping, took on the form of an eagle once more and pursued them on his powerful wings. He came closer and closer, yet each time he tried to strike down the smaller birds Loki darted away, out of reach of the eagle's talons.

As the chase neared Asgard, the gods were standing side by side on the city walls and their hearts filled with fear when they saw the huge eagle poised to destroy the tired falcon and tiny swallow. With a last effort, Loki fluttered in through a little window in the palace wall. Thiassi was too big to follow and beat the air outside in vain. This moment was enough for Thor, the god of thunder, to hurl a thunderbolt at him. Blinded, and with his feathers afire, Thiassi plunged to his death on the rocks below.

The gods of Asgard rejoiced that Iduna was safe among them. She became her beautiful self once more and the hazel nut was transformed into the golden casket. Soon the apples of youth restored to the gods their strength and happiness. While everyone celebrated her return, Iduna smiled down on the earth and it became greener and more lovely than ever before.

Question box

Why does Loki help to kidnap Iduna?
What happens to the gods after Iduna disappears?
Where does Thiassi take Iduna?
Which birds are mentioned in this story?
When does Loki use his talent for trickery?

How might Bragi have discovered Loki's guilt?
Why do you think Loki offered to rescue Iduna?
Do you think it was fair that Thor killed Thiassi?
Did Loki deserve to be punished or rewarded?
Who, other than the gods, benefits from Iduna's return?

Exploring ideas

1 Out in the cold

The gods would want to hear what had happened to Iduna while she had been in Thiassi's power. They know nothing of her experiences after the kidnap.

Write, from Iduna's point of view, the story of the lonely and frightening events.

2 Here comes summer!

The story finishes: 'Iduna smiled down on the earth and it became greener and more lovely than ever before.'

Imagine that you are standing on the walls of Asgard at that moment, and describe everything you see as these changes take place.

3 A gift from the gods?

You have <u>one</u> of the following magic powers:
    A magic pocket that is always full of whatever you want.
    The ability to read people's thoughts.
    The power to turn everything into gold.
    The power to know the future but not be able to change it.

Write about what happens to you as a result of having this power. What might the disadvantages be? Make it clear if you are happier or unhappier at the end.

4 Weigh it up

The 'pros' and 'cons' of any argument are the reasons **for** and **against**. Here is an example of the reasons for and against watching television.

Watching television	
pros	cons
Relaxing	Wastes times
Broadens the mind	Tires the eyes
Full of good ideas	Kills conversation
Brings the family together	Causes arguments
Something to look forward to	Something you can't escape
Good for watching sport	Stops participation in sport
Keeps people in touch with events	Makes human suffering seem unreal
Advertises new products	Persuades people to buy things they don't need

Do you think all these points are fair?

The gods were very keen to stay young. Would **you** like to take some special tablet to stay your present age? Make a table of the pros and cons for this idea.

5 Plots and plans!

Imagine that you want to kidnap somebody. Describe your plan carefully and practically, and then describe your attempt. (Remember: you are not gods or gangsters! Make sure your plot uses things that you could obtain.)

In your plan you will need:
a) A reason for the kidnap
b) A way of luring the person to the right spot
c) A means of transport
d) A secret hiding place
e) A means of getting from them what you want

In the story of the attempt you should say:
a) Whether your plot worked
b) What happened at the end

6 Ever been had?

There are lots of words meaning 'to trick'. Some of them are used more often than others.

If you have been tricked, you might feel that you have been bamboozled, or beguiled, or cheated, or conned, or deceived, or diddled, or done, or duped, or hoodwinked, or hornswoggled, or ripped-off, or swindled, or even taken for a ride! There are so many words for trickery that you can see it happens in many ways and in many situations.

Have you ever conned someone or been diddled yourself? Write an account in which *either* you are the person who is tricked, *or* you trick someone else.

Discovering words

Learn the language

Here is a piece of writing that describes part of the story:

> The gods were *cross* when they discovered Loki's *bad* secret. They spoke in an *unkind* way to him and called him *naughty*. Bragi was *sad* while Thor looked *big* and *nasty*. Loki tried to explain his *poor* deeds and said he would search for Iduna and her *special, nice* apples.

Although these sentences tell us what happened, they do not give a very gripping account of the incident. Rewrite this passage replacing the words in italic type with stronger and more descriptive ones.

Either take the words from the list below, or choose your own. You should use a dictionary to check any meanings.

appalling	gigantic	outraged	terrible
desolate	hostile	precious	treacherous
despicable	massive	remarkable	unique
evil	menacing	ruthless	wicked
furious	miserable	savage	wonderful

Watch your step

It's and *its* have different meanings:

It's = *it is*.
Its = *of it*.

If *it is* does not make sense, then it must be *its*.

Here is the kidnapping plot that Thiassi revealed to Loki. Copy it out, deciding whether *it's* or *its* fits the gaps.

> 'Listen, Loki, ... a plan which will even fool the gods! ... success depends, however, upon Iduna believing that ... safe to leave Asgard and venture outside ... walls. Make sure that she brings the golden casket, because ... ... wonderful contents, not just her, that I really want!
> I shall be waiting outside the city, disguised as an eagle. ... strong wings will help me to make my escape, and ... a good

way to avoid suspicion. From that moment ... up to me. The casket will reward me with ... powers.'

Try a new way

If you want to change a story into a play, you need to write a script. This will tell the actors what to say, how to say it, and when to enter or leave the stage. You need to include a cast list, give stage directions, and provide any other instructions. Here is a short example of part of *The Apples of Iduna* written in the form of a play.

Cast: Iduna
          Loki
Scene: Inside the palace of Asgard

(Iduna is seated, the golden casket beside her. Loki peers round the door, smiles wickedly, and enters the room.)

Iduna: (cheerfully) Good morning, Loki. What a lovely day!

Loki: It's all thanks to your marvellous apples. No wonder you sound happy.

Iduna: Thank you, Loki. I am glad I can help to keep the gods young.

Loki: (cunningly) So am I . . . but *I* know where there are even finer apples!

Iduna: (puzzled) What do you mean?

Now write your own script. You can either continue this episode or choose a different part of the story. You could choose the passage where the gods are in their palace, growing old and miserable without Iduna's apples.

Or you could choose the part where Bragi discovers Loki's guilt. Try and think of a clever way in which Bragi, like a detective, could catch Loki out.

Or you could choose the episode in which Thiassi, in the cold cave, tries to force Iduna to give *him* immortality. Imagine how frightened, but determined, she would be.

Magic apple quizword

Find the words from the story.

Iduna's apple

1. it was Loki who had ___ Iduna
2. the beautiful goddess of ___
3. Seizing the terrified goddess and her ___ casket
4. ill ___ and old age
5. ___ from the Tree of Life
6. The Palace of ___ now seemed silent and sad
7. he would help to trap Iduna and her golden ___

Loki's apple

1. Loki, the ___-making god
2. ___ himself in the shape of a falcon
3. he begged to be given the chance to ___ the goddess.
4. he knew of an ___ beyond the city walls
5. he clutched her firmly in his ___ claws
6. Loki used his magic powers to change her into a ___

Thiassi's apple

1. the people lived among ___ mountains and gloomy forests.
2. Blinded, and with his feathers ___
3. pursued them on his ___ wings.
4. plunged to his ___ on the rocks
5. Thiassi saw them escaping, took on the form of an ___
6. poised to ___ the tired falcon

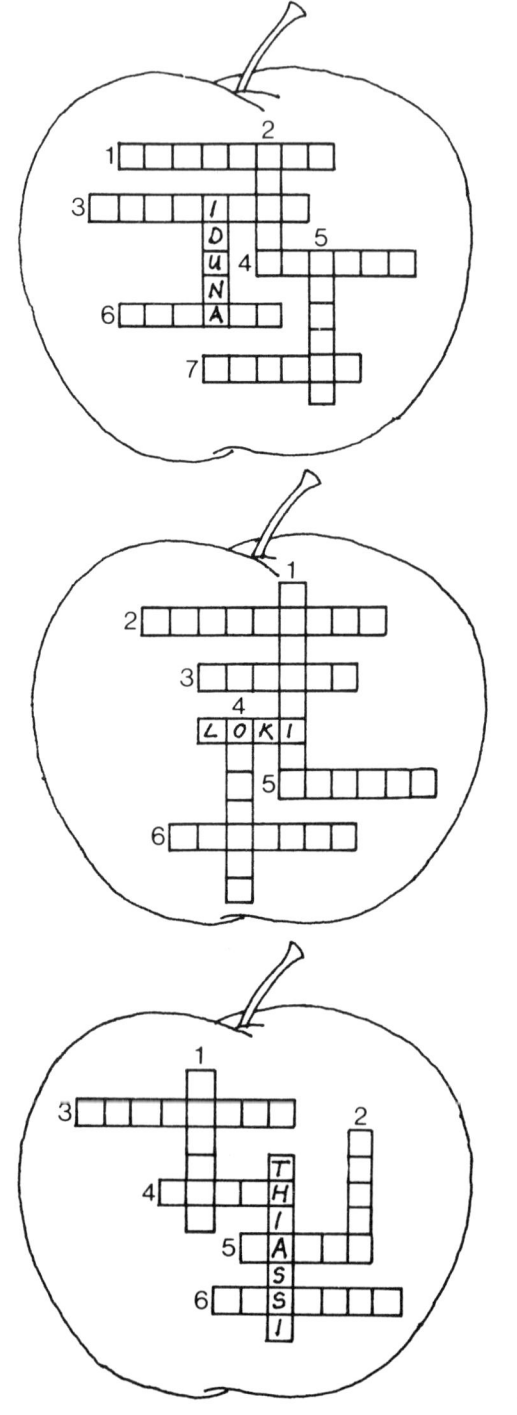

The world of Iduna

The story comes from the Norse people of Scandinavia. Summer is very brief in the cold, northern lands and the Norse valued it very highly. Giants and dwarfs were part of their explanation of the dangers that always threatened.

Who's in it?

Iduna ....the goddess who guards the apples of youth
Bragi ....a god, Iduna's husband
Loki ....the mischief-making god
Thiassi ......the storm giant
Thor ....the god of thunder
Other gods and giants

What happens?

1. Iduna provides apples of youth for the gods.
2. Thiassi plots to kidnap Iduna.
3. Loki betrays Iduna by luring her to the orchard.
4. Thiassi, disguised as an eagle, captures and imprisons her.
5. The gods grow old without the apples of youth.
6. Bragi discovers Loki's guilt.
7. Loki searches for Iduna until he finds her.
8. They set off in disguise but Thiassi pursues them.
9. Thor kills Thiassi with a thunderbolt.
10. The gods regain their youth.

Step into the drama world

Despite trickery and threats, Iduna refuses to forget her friends.

Step one   A clever lie deceives her.
Step two   She resists pressure to betray her trust.
Step three Disguise proves to be useful.
Step four One person's return solves all the problems.

And it *can* happen now . . . . .

Step one

Sit in a circle

Everyone should think of something unusual that has, or could have, happened to him or her. It might be true, or it might be false. It must be told so that it *sounds* like the truth.
At the end of each 'story', the others may ask questions which the speaker must answer. Everyone will then vote to show if they think the story was true or false. The truth will then be revealed.
Listen to several stories.

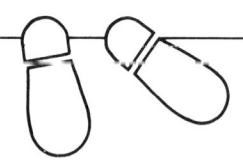

Step two

Find a partner A and B

A is a bankrobber.   B is a bank clerk.
A had kidnapped B in order to find out the combination of the safe, which B knows.
While trying to discover this number, A may use persuasion but must never actually *touch* B.
B wants to remain loyal to his employers and would like A to understand this. He does not wish to make A angry.
                        What happens?

Step three

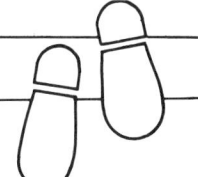

Groups of three/four

One of the group (X) is a famous personality. X is staying at a hotel, and does not want to be recognized or interviewed.
A newspaper has sent reporters and a photographer to the hotel to get an interview with X.
X will disguise his/her voice and appearance in order to leave the hotel. The reporters are suspicious and ask a lot of questions.
                    Do they discover who it is?

Step four

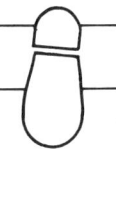

Groups of four/five

You are a group of explorers in a remote part of the world.
Something happens that means that the doctor of the group disappears. (Lost? Kidnapped?)
A series of accidents happen and the doctor is needed. Everyone becomes worried and upset.
At last the doctor returns to the expedition.
How do the explorers feel about his return?
                    Can he improve matters?

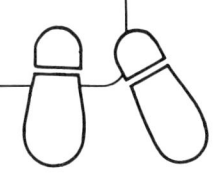

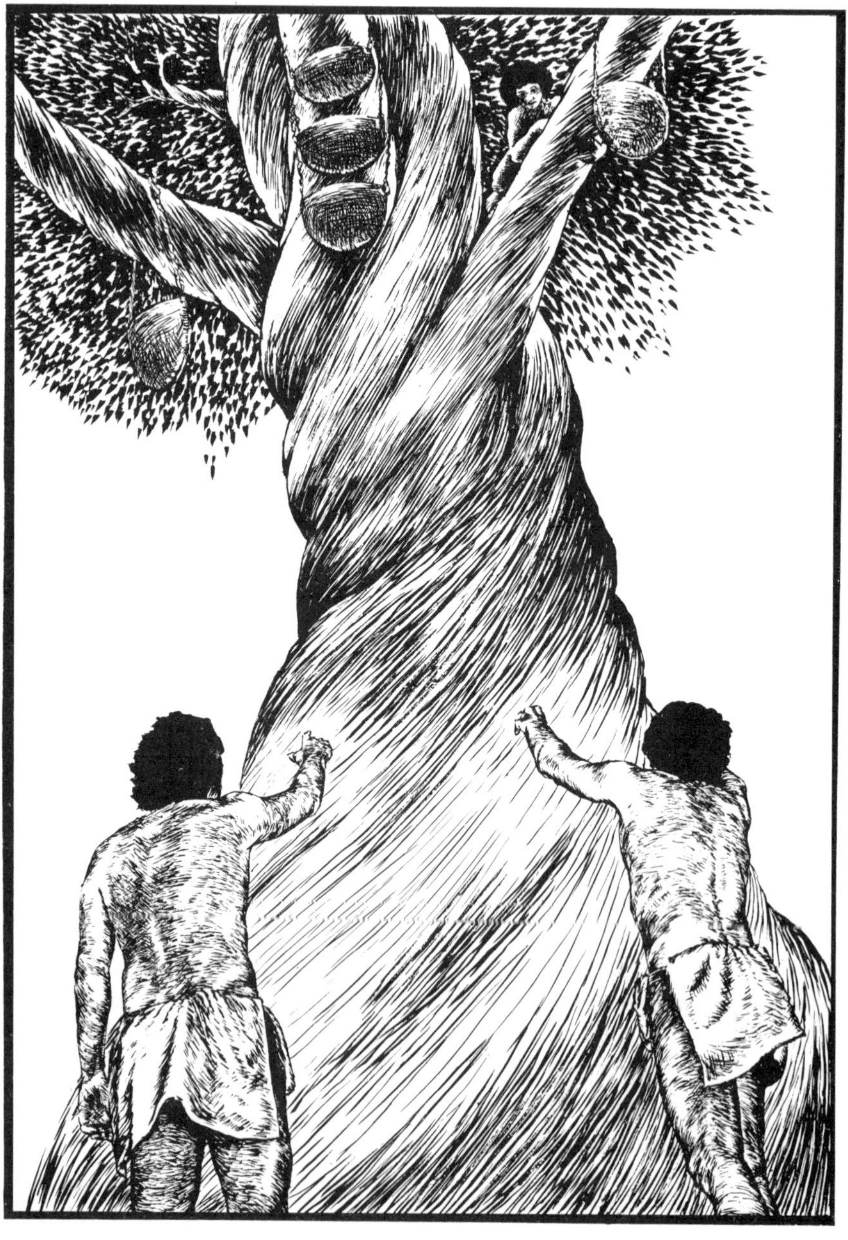

3 The world of cruelty

The Day the Creek went Dry

There was once a little boy whose mother and father died when he was still very small. The tribe he lived with were not kind to him. Everyone believed he brought bad luck because his parents had both died, and so they ignored him and gave him no love.

At this time water was scarce everywhere. Nobody would give Kooh-Borr any; it was as though they wished that he too were dead.

One day the whole tribe, under their leader Pund-Jel, went out hunting. As usual, they left Kooh-Borr behind. However, they had forgotten to hang up their wooden drinking-bowls, which were called coolamons, so for once Kooh-Borr had enough to drink. Because he was angry at the way the tribe had treated him, and so that he might never be without water again, Kooh-Borr took all the coolamons and hung them on the boughs of a little tree. Then he scooped all the water out of the creek and put it into the coolamons, climbing up beside them. As he settled himself in the tree, he shook the branches and some water spilt and soaked into the roots. Suddenly the tree grew very tall and lifted Kooh-Borr high above the ground.

In the evening the tribe returned from their hunting. They had caught nothing and the day had been hot so the people were very thirsty. But they could not find their coolamons anywhere in the camp. Several tribesmen went to the creek, thinking the coolamons might be there: it was then that they realized that the creek was dry.

Presently, one of the men noticed a huge new tree. At his shout, all the others turned to look and there they could see their coolamons hanging high up, with little Kooh-Borr perched among them. Pund-Jel shouted loudly to Kooh-Borr, telling him to let them have some water, but Kooh-Borr said he would not give the tribe a single drop because they had not given him any when he had been nearly dying of thirst.

Two of the strongest men were so thirsty that they started to climb the tree, although they were frightened of its height. Kooh-Borr laughed and let a little water fall on them. They tried to catch the cool water in their mouths but their fingers became slippery and they fell to the ground and were killed. More and more men tried to climb to the branch where Kooh-Borr sat but the same thing happened to them.

At last Ta-Jerr and Taarn-Nin, the two sons of Pund-Jel, thought of a plan. While they climbed, they moved round and round the trunk of the tree in the same way as a creeping plant would do. Kooh-Borr laughed at them too until they were far above the ground, when he took water and let it drop as before. But the men were no longer in the same place and the water missed them.

Kooh-Borr fetched more water, pouring it where he had last seen the men, but again it did not touch them and at last Ta-Jerr and Taarn-Nin reached the safe branches. Little Kooh-Borr began to cry but the two men took no notice. They seized him and beat him until all his bones became quite soft. Then they threw him down to the other tribesmen who tried to kill him. But instead of dying, Kooh-Borr changed into what he is now – the koala bear – and ran up another tree to hide.

Ta-Jerr and Taarn-Nin cut down the big tree and the water flowed out and filled the creek. The tribe did not hunt Kooh-Borr because they knew they had treated him badly.

The koala bear always keeps near the banks of creeks so that he can carry the water away if ever the people are unkind to him again. But since this time no-one has ever roasted the koala without his skin or broken his bones in killing him. When anyone climbs a tree in which the koala is sitting, he always cries in the same manner as Kooh-Borr cried when Ta-Jerr and Taarn-Nin climbed the great tree.

Question box

Why did the tribe not like Kooh-Borr?
Why was the tribe thirsty when they returned from hunting in the evening?
Why did the strong men fall to the ground?
How did the sons of Pund-Jel climb the tree?
How did they show they were cross with Kooh-Borr?

How was the tribe unkind to Kooh-Borr?
How did Kooh-Borr make sure that the tribe would have no water?
Why do you think Kooh-Borr changed into the koala bear?
How did the tribe show they were sorry that they had been cruel to Kooh-Borr?
How does the koala bear still remind us of Kooh-Borr?

Exploring ideas

1 All alone

We do not know how Kooh-Borr's mother and father died when he was still very small. Perhaps he lost his parents in an unexpected and tragic way. Make up your own explanation as to how Kooh-Borr became an orphan.

2 A lot to answer for?

If one of the Aborigines told a member of another tribe about Kooh-Borr, he would make him sound very unpleasant. Everything that had ever gone wrong would be blamed on the orphan boy.

Try and list as many things as you can from this different point of view, in order to make Kooh-Borr sound like the real villain of the story. Invent details of misfortunes such as illnesses and bad weather, that you could say were all Kooh-Borr's fault.

3 Raw deal

The last part of the story tells how the koala bear came to be frightened of people. There are many creatures in the world that are hunted, eaten, or kept in captivity by man.

Choose an animal that you believe is treated in a cruel way. Try and imagine what it would think of human beings. The creature might not understand what was happening, but it would understand fear.

Write a view of its life, as seen through the animal's eyes.

4 Water, please!

Imagine your world with no water for *just one week*. You can invent your own reason why this is so. In your home you might still have milk, lemonade, beer or any other liquid. . .but NO WATER.

Write your 'DIARY' for this week describing all the problems you face, both indoors and outdoors. Make it very clear why you are so glad when the water-shortage is over at the end of the week.

5 How on earth?

The story of Kooh-Borr gives an explanation for the first koala bear. There are a lot of other unusual animals found in the world, not just in Australia. Kangaroos, giraffes, elephants, and many other species all have remarkable features. It is tempting to explain the origin of such creatures in terms of a human being who looked strange, or had peculiar habits. For some reason, this person might have been changed into an animal.

Choose an unusual animal and make up a tale to explain how it came to exist.

6 Help yourself

You are trapped, by the incoming tide, at the foot of a steep cliff. Before you came for a walk on the beach, you had been shopping for some fairly unusual items. These are all safely packed in a carrier bag that you still have with you. They might include:

a packet of balloons
a pair of double sheets
six can pack of lemonade
assortment of fireworks
a crepe bandage
a box of cutlery
a pair of high-heeled shoes
a rugby ball
a bottle of nail varnish

Unfortunately, nothing in the bag seems to be *obviously* useful to help you to save yourself. You realize, however, that you are on your own, and no-one is about to rescue you. You have a brilliant idea! Some of the things in the bag, used cleverly, could mean that an amazing escape is possible. Just the thing for the local paper!

List the items in the carrier bag. Then write the report, giving it a striking headline of your own choice.

Discovering words

Try a new way

The story of Kooh-Borr is told in quite a straightforward way. If we wanted to make certain parts of the story even more exciting or colourful, we could use **similes**.

Similes are *imaginative* comparisons that usually start with *like* or *as*.

Here are some examples:

    The creek looked *like a dead snake*.
    Kooh-Borr ran *like the wind*.
    Kooh-Borr ran *as if devils were after him*.

See if you can complete any of these sentences with similes that fit in with the story, and sound interesting.

1 Kooh-Borr was as lonely as ....
2 Pund-Jel shouted in a voice like ....
3 All the men were as thirsty as ....
4 Little Kooh-Borr began to cry like ....
5 The big tree fell to the ground as if ....
6 The sun felt as hot as ....

Can you think of any other parts of the story where **similes** would make some detail more vivid?

Write them down in sentences.

Learn the language

The story is full of action. Every time anything happens, some word always describes exactly what the action is:

The tree *grows*.
Pund-Jel *shouts*.
The men *fell*.
Kooh-Borr *cries*.

1 There are more than SIXTY **action-words** in the story!
    How many can you find? Write them down in a list.

2 Choose TEN of these **action-words** and put them into sentences about yourself.

3 Can you think of any other words that have nearly the same meaning as any of those you have found?
For example:

shouts = yells = bawls = screams
fell = tumbled = dropped = plummeted
cries = sobs = weeps = howls

4 Rewrite any sentences from the story where you can change the action-word, putting a new word in its place.

Read the signs

When people are excited, or talking to close friends, they sometimes use *slang*. This can be colourful and amusing, but it can also be ugly or confusing.

You should **never** put slang in your writing, unless you are trying to record the actual speech that someone has used.

Here is what a hunter might have said about Kooh-Borr, if he had told his story in slang!

> 'My mates and I were out trying to rustle up a spot of grub. It was one heck of a scorcher and what a thirst I had on me! We caught nothing, so we had a bit of a rabbit among ourselves and then packed it in. We hoofed it back to our hang-out, ready to hit the sack, but, strike me pink, the river had hopped it.
> I thought my peepers were playing me up. One of our blokes, it might have been the boss or my old man, copped sight of a kid up a tree. This little squirt had nicked our water. He started blabbing out a mouthful of cheek. Would he button his lip? Sling his hook? No way! What he needed was a good belt. The creep didn't give a hoot if we snuffed it, so I was chuffed when this beefy geezer nipped up the tree. The little twerp had had his chips!'

Rewrite this speech, avoiding the slang. Be careful not to change the meaning.

Coolamon quizword

Find the words from the story.

Kooh-Borr's coolamon

1. Everyone believed he brought ___ (2 words)
2. he was ___ at the way the tribe had treated him.
3. They seized him and ___ him.
4. Kooh-Borr changed into what he is now – the ___ (2 words)
5. no-one has ever roasted the koala without his ___.
6. their wooden drinking bowls, which were called ___.
7. water was ___ everywhere.
8. They tried to catch the cool ___.
9. hung them on the boughs of a little ___.
10. Suddenly the tree ___ very tall

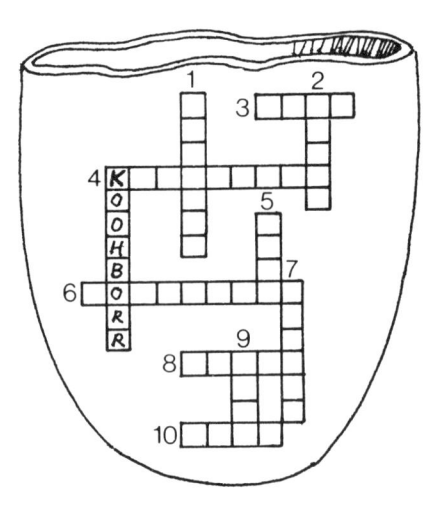

Pund-Jel's coolamon

1. they realized that the creek was ___.
2. In the evening the ___ returned
3. the day had been hot so the people were very ___.
4. the water flowed out and filled the ___.
5. When anyone ___ a tree
6. they fell to the ground and were ___
7. One day the whole tribe ...... went out ___.
8. under their ___ Pund-Jel
9. While they climbed, they moved ___
10. Pund-Jel ___ loudly to Kooh-Borr

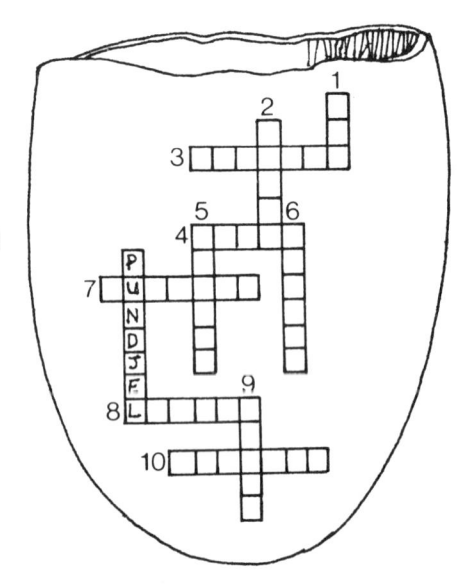

38

The world of Kooh-Borr

The Aborigines of Australia tell many stories of the 'Dream-Time' when the world was young and life began. This story of the origin of the koala was told by the people of the Upper Yarra river area in south-east Australia.

Who's in it?

Kooh-Borr .... an Aboriginal boy who is an orphan
Pund-Jel .... the leader of the tribe
Ta-Jerr and Taarn-Nin .... his sons
Other members of the tribe

What happens?

1 Kooh-Borr is treated badly by the tribe.
2 While the tribe are away hunting, he hides all the water in a tree.
3 Some water spills when he sits in the tree, and it grows tall.
4 The tribe return to find the creek dry.
5 Because Kooh-Borr refuses to give them any water, some men try to climb the tree.
6 Kooh-Borr pours water on them, making them fall to their deaths.
7 The leader's sons succeed in climbing the tree.
8 They beat Kooh-Borr and throw him down.
9 The little boy changes into a koala bear.
10 The tree is cut down and the water fills the creek.

Step into the drama world

The tribe are cruel to Kooh-Borr, and so he tries to hurt them in return.

Step one   He is lonely and unhappy.
Step two   He hides something that others need.
Step three A trick gets out of hand.
Step four The others realize that they have been unfair to him.

And it *can* happen now . . . . .

Step one

Stand in a space

You cannot move from this spot. You feel lonely and unhappy. You are very angry with everyone. Your face should show your feelings. If the teacher touches your shoulder, you are free to move around the room, and your anger disappears. Walk near the others, showing them how happy **you** feel. Enjoy meeting everyone, but do not speak to, or touch, anyone. If the teacher taps you on the shoulder again, you must stand still and become lonely and unhappy again.

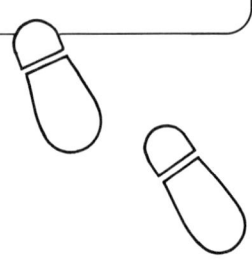

Step two

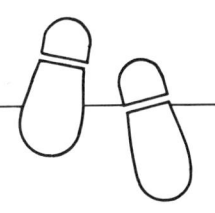

Find a partner A and B

A has hidden B's front door key. He enjoys teasing B, who is desperate to get his key back. B tries every method of pleading, persuasion and threats except force. What happens?

Step three

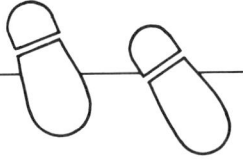

Groups of three A, B and C

You are visiting a house which is supposed to be haunted. A decides it would be fun to frighten B and C. He pretends to see ghosts and make strange noises occur. When B and C discover that they have been tricked, they turn on A. They tie him up and leave him trapped in the house alone.

Step four

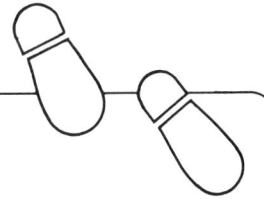

Groups of four/five.

One person needs to volunteer to be X.
You are a group of people who live or work together. X is not liked by the others for some silly little reason.
They show their dislike of X in the things that they do and say, but they may not say anything that is directly unpleasant.
Finally, the group will realize that they have been unfair to X. They will try to be especially nice to him to make up for their earlier unfriendliness. It is up to X to decide whether this makes things better.

Act it.

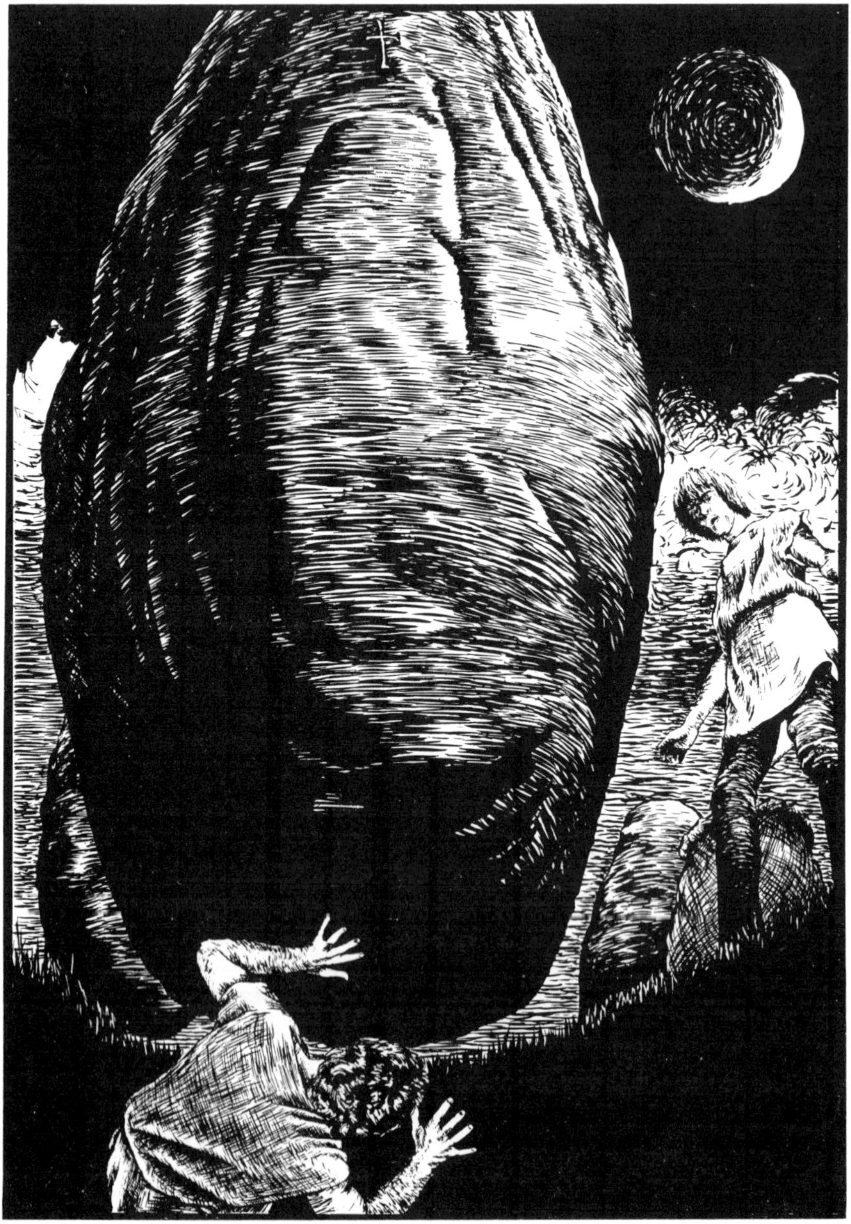

4 The world of mysteries

The Seven Black Stones

Many hundreds of years ago, in the small village of Plouhinec, lived a young man named Bernez. He was a skilful stone-mason, but poor because he could not find work.

Near the village lay a desolate heath, in the middle of which stood seven black stones. All were bigger than a man and one hundred-ton stone stood twenty feet high. The villagers feared the great stones, which they thought watched people who passed nearby and whispered in an evil way.

Bernez, who was a Christian, was not afraid of these strange stones. When he went looking for work, he often walked between them. One day he even placed his ladder against the largest stone, climbed up, and then cut a cross into its granite face. Suddenly he heard his name called. For a moment Bernez thought that the stone had spoken, but then he realized that it was a ragged beggar standing below.

The beggar taunted Bernez because he was too poor to marry the girl he loved. With a cunning smile, he told the stone-mason that they could easily obtain a great treasure which was near at hand, if only Bernez would help him.

The beggar said that every hundred years, during the night of the longest day, the laws of nature changed: things that had been fixed were set free, while all other creatures lost the power to move. Only a man holding a four-leaf clover would be unchanged. At midnight, the stones would rise up and walk to the river to drink, and that man could find a marvellous treasure in the pit of the largest stone.

Now the beggar smiled sweetly at Bernez, who knew the heath so well, and asked him to find a four-leaf clover as it was Midsummer's Day. If Bernez helped him to obtain the treasure, he could share it and be rich enough to marry. Although he did not believe his story, Bernez felt pity for the beggar and agreed. The man thanked him and went away, laughing to himself. During the afternoon, the stone-mason searched the heath carefully until, many hours later, he found some of the rare plants.

That night, Bernez and the beggar, each holding tightly a four-leaf clover, went to the stones and sat waiting for midnight. As the village clock struck the first note of twelve, incredibly the beggar's words came true. Impossible things happened. Living creatures were frozen in their movement; even the birds hung in mid-flight. Then slowly, one by one, the great stones began to rise up and move towards the river.

The beggar signalled to Bernez to follow him to the pit where the largest stone had stood. Here they saw, to their delight, a wonderful hoard of gold and jewels. Quickly the beggar leapt into the hole. He began to pass the treasure up to Bernez, who put it into some sacks they had brought.

Suddenly the beggar jumped out of the hole and pointed to the river. Bernez gasped as he saw the great stones lumbering back. As he stared in awe, the beggar dashed forward and knocked the four-leaf clover from his hand. Immediately the poor stone-mason could not move. The beggar laughed in his face and mocked him. He told Bernez that he had made an evil bargain with the stones, promising them human blood in exchange for their treasure.

Now Bernez realized what a fool he had been, but he could do nothing. The huge stones were all sliding back into their sockets and the greatest stone of all was lurching steadily towards him. At any moment he expected to be crushed under its terrible weight.

Suddenly the stone halted and Bernez could just make out the small cross he had carved high up in the dark granite. The beggar rushed at the stone, screaming at it to crush Bernez, but it did not move. In his fury, the beggar beat the great stone with his fists and, at that moment, the four-leaf clover slipped from his grasp. For a second he stood frozen and then he toppled backwards into the pit. Now the stone moved once more and, gently avoiding Bernez, ground its huge weight down onto the beggar and was still.

The clock struck the second note of twelve. Living creatures were free to move again and Bernez looked around in a daze. Everything looked as it had before. Then Bernez saw the bulging sacks full of treasure and he knew that he had not been dreaming. Now he would never be poor again and he could at last marry his true love.

> **Question box**
>
> Why did Bernez cut a cross in a stone?
> When were the stones supposed to move?
> How did Bernez help the beggar?
> What had to be exchanged for the treasure?
> Why did the beggar drop his clover-leaf?
>
> What was frightening about the stones?
> In what ways did Bernez not have a happy life?
> Does the beggar ever act suspiciously?
> How do we know that time stands still in this story?
> Why do you think the stone crushed the beggar rather than Bernez?

Exploring ideas

1 Well I never!

Bernez, who had been poor, suddenly became rich. But who in Plouhinec would believe his story? Imagine that you are one of the villagers and say how you think Bernez might have found his wealth.

2 Impossible things happened . . .

On the first stroke of midnight, 'living creatures were frozen in their movement; even the birds hung in mid-flight'. What would you have actually *seen* if you had been there at this magic moment?

Think of details like:

a) The creatures that might have been there, and their appearance when they lost the power to move.
b) What happened to things that could not normally move.

Use your imagination and describe in writing what you could have seen when 'impossible things happened'.

3 X-certificate?

It is quite frightening when Bernez is threatened by things that are not 'flesh and blood'. The stones can kill without any mercy.

If the furniture, machines, and other things in your own home could move, they might try to trap you.

Imagine that you come home from school one evening and this happens. This sounds like a real horror story. So write it . . .

4 Living legends

The Seven Black Stones is a *legend*: a story that has been told for many years and may have some truth to it.

Some people believe that the seven stones of Plouhinec are the last survivors of a Roman legion, who were magically turned to stone.

All we actually *know* about the stones is:
- there are seven of them;
- they stand quite close together;
- they are found on a desolate heath;
- one is much larger than the others.

Use some, or all, of these facts when you create your own legend, to explain how the seven stones of Plouhinec come to be there.

5 Yours faithfully

A stone-mason can work on houses and churches, carve elaborate tombstones, or make monuments.

Imagine that you are Bernez and you are looking for work. You have to write to somebody who is thinking of employing a mason. Include all the *details* of what you can do and explain how skilful you have been in past jobs.

Set the beginning of the letter out as follows:

Carver's Cottage,
Heath Road,
Plouhinec,
Brittany

1st May, 1283

Dear Sir,
    I hear that you are in need of a good stone-mason.
I would like to tell you about work that I have done recently.

---

6 Never again

Greed is very ugly. It can ruin someone's life. It might be greed for food, for money, or for anything else. Perhaps you know someone who has been made miserable through greed. Otherwise you can easily imagine it.
Write a story where awful things happen to a person because he or she is so greedy.

Discovering words

Watch your step

> WARNING! ALL TREASURE TROVE MUST BE DECLARED TO THE KING. ANY PERSON FINDING TREASURE MUST PREPARE A LIST OF ALL VALUABLES IN STRICT ALPHABETICAL ORDER, OR THAT PERSON WILL LOSE HIS TREASURE AND HIS HEAD!

Bernez found:
diamonds, golden cups, rubies, ivory, silver plates, amethysts, gold ingots, emeralds, rings, bronze jugs, jet, necklaces, jade, pearls, brooches, quartz, silver bracelets, gold coins, sapphires, opals.

Sort out this list into alphabetical order.

Learn the language

When Bernez and the beggar are waiting for midnight, they hold the clover *tightly*.

This word '*tightly*' tells us *how* they are holding the clover. Think how a different word would give you a different picture of what they are doing:
> They held the clover *loosely/furiously/sadly*.

a) There are at least TEN other words in the story that end in -ly, and tell us *how* something is being done. See if you can find them and write them down.

b) Sometimes an -ly word has to be chosen very carefully:
The great stones lumbered *delicately* to the river. (This sounds wrong.)
The great stones lumbered *clumsily/heavily/ponderously* to the river.
Which word works best?

c) The sentences below contain words that tell us *how* something was done. These words need to be replaced with more suitable ones.

1. Bernez stood cheerfully frozen to the spot.
2. The seven stones towered feebly over them.
3. The beggar swore politely at Bernez.
4. He threw the treasure casually out of the pit.
5. The beggar cried out happily as he was crushed by the great stone.

Write the sentences out, changing the word that describes *how* things happened to a word that fits better.

Read the signs

It is strange how often the number *seven* crops up. In fact it is rather mysterious! Try to solve the mystery of these *sevens*.

1. What would you be able to do if you wore SEVEN LEAGUE BOOTS?
2. If you were the SEVENTH CHILD OF A SEVENTH CHILD what gift would you possess?
3. In which town would you find SEVEN SISTERS and SEVEN DIALS?
4. In which city would you be if you found it stood on SEVEN HILLS?
5. Who or what is each of the SEVEN DAYS OF THE WEEK named after?
6. If you sailed the SEVEN SEAS, where would your ship travel?
7. Who would you have had to fight if you had been challenged by the SEVEN CHAMPIONS OF CHRISTENDOM?
8. If you had the SEVEN DEADLY SINS what would your faults be?
9. When and where would you have lived if you had been involved in the SEVEN YEARS' WAR?
10. If you had visited the SEVEN WONDERS OF THE ANCIENT WORLD, where would you have gone and what would you have seen?
11. If you were Snow White and wanted to invite the SEVEN DWARFS to your wedding, what names would you write on the seven invitations?

Four-leaf clover quizword

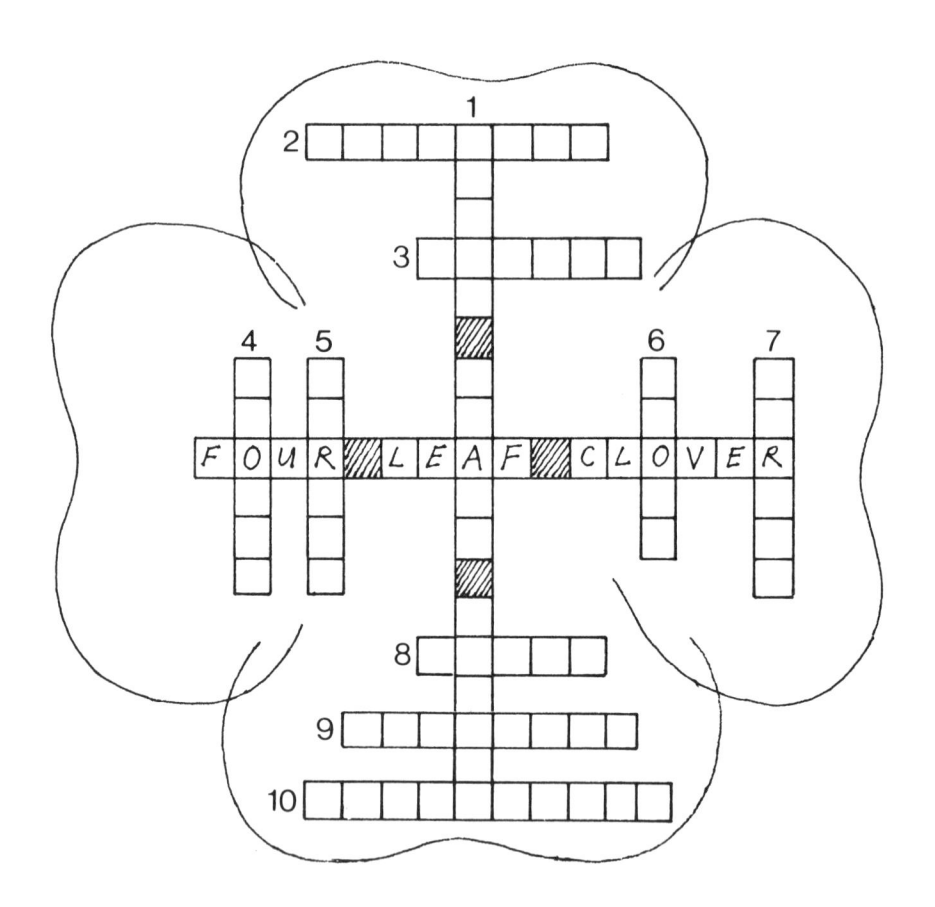

Find the words from the story.

1. a desolate heath, in the middle of which stood ___ . (3 words)
2. that man could find a marvellous ___
3. he realized that it was a ragged ___
4. Living creatures were ___ in their movement
5. ___ thought that the stone had spoken.
6. then cut a ___ into its granite face.
7. he had ___ it high up in the dark granite.
8. ground its huge weight down onto the beggar, and was ___ .
9. went to the stones and sat waiting for ___ .
10. ___ things happened.

The world of Bernez

This story comes from Brittany in France where there are many stone circles and lines of stones. Some people believe that they are connected with ancient religion or astronomy. Legends have grown up around them and some still believe that the stones retain mysterious secrets.

Who's in it?

Bernez............a young stone-mason

The beggar.....a mysterious, ragged stranger

The seven black stones

What happens?

1. Bernez, a poor stone-mason, carves a cross on a huge black stone.
2. A ragged beggar tells Bernez the legend of the stones.
3. He promises Bernez great wealth if he will help by finding some four-leaf clovers.
4. Bernez searches the heath until he finds them.
5. At midnight, Bernez and the beggar wait near the circle of stones.
6. As the clock strikes, everything changes and the stones move.
7. Bernez and the beggar collect the treasure from the pit where the large stone stood.
8. As the stones return, the beggar tricks Bernez so that he cannot move.
9. The stone spares Bernez but crushes the beggar.
10. Things return to normal and Bernez has the treasure.

Step into the drama world

Bernez becomes involved in a strange adventure, and is lucky to escape death.

Step one   A thing is supposed to move when no-one can see it.
Step two   Bernez gives assistance to someone who needs help.
Step three   He becomes caught up in a dangerous adventure.
Step four   Everything that happens seems very unreal.

And it *can* happen now . . . . .

Step one

Make a big circle

One person, X, stands in the middle. People forming the circle stand like stones, stiff and still. These 'stones' will try to reach X without being seen to move. They must stay totally silent, and may only take *very* tiny steps. If X sees one of the 'stones' moving, he will point at it. That stone will then stand frozen, and will show this by crossing its arms on its chest. Any stone reaching X will take his place.

The circle will then re-form.

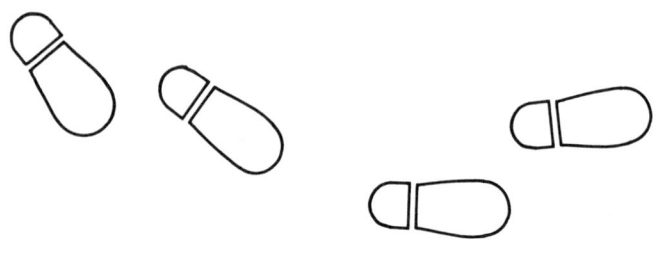

Step two

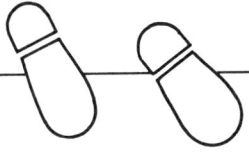

Find a partner A and B

A must keep his eyes completely closed and put his trust in B. B holds A's wrist gently, and guides him slowly around the room in any direction, not letting him bump into anything. No-one may speak. At any point B may let go of A's wrist. When this happens, A must stand totally frozen, eyes still closed, until B takes hold again to lead him on.

Later, A will lead B.

Step three

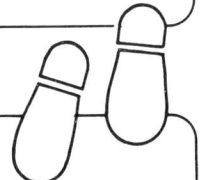

Groups of three A, B and C

A asks B to help do something that may be dangerous. C gives good reasons why B should not help. B ignores this advice, and goes with A. C joins them because he suspects A of being up to no good.

Is C right?

Step four

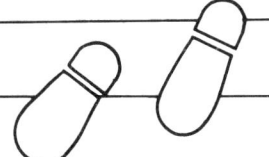

Groups of four/five.

Call one of the group X.

In the morning X gets up. He meets people going to school, or work, or out shopping. At first, little things seem strange, and then X realizes that a great deal of what is happening is very mysterious or disturbing. For example, X may meet friends who do not seem to know him, *or* people appear to be speaking and he cannot make out what they are saying, *or* X is told amazing things that he finds almost impossible to believe.

At some point, everyone except X will freeze in position. It has all been a dream.

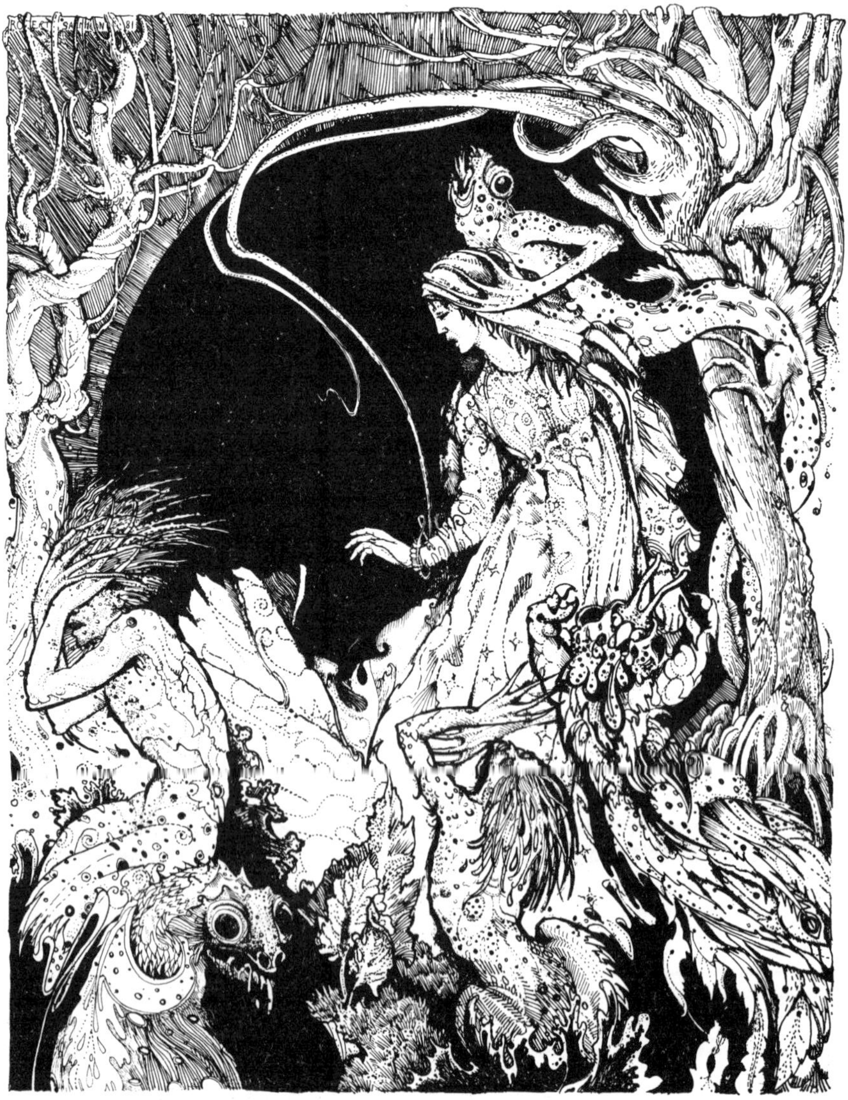

5 The world of darkness

The Dead Moon

Long ago, Lincolnshire had vast fens which were impossible to cross after dark, except on moonlit nights. For when the Moon was not shining, Dead Things and Nightmare Horrors crawled around, spreading harm and misfortune.

The Moon heard how bad things were when she turned her back and she decided to discover for herself if she could help. So, when the month ended, she wrapped herself in a black cloak, with a black hood to conceal her shining hair, and stepped down into the dark marsh-lands. As the Moon walked deeper across the quagmire, the Horrors slid out from their hiding-holes. Will-o'-the-wisps looped like moths; dead fingers beckoned and clutched from the foul water. Suddenly, the Moon's foot sank down and she caught at a branch to hold her balance. As soon as the branch was touched, it twisted like a rope and trapped her by the wrists. In vain she fought to free herself, until she had to pause for breath. Then, faintly, she heard a frightened voice and she knew that a man was lost in the darkness.

Soon she could see him. Led astray by a will-o'-the-wisp, he was stumbling dangerously towards the waiting Horrors. The Moon was so angry that she struggled hard again, until her hood slipped off. At once the light streamed from her silver hair, showing the safe path to the man. He staggered towards it, while the Evil Things cowered from the hated moonlight.

At last, however, the Moon dropped exhausted to her knees and the black hood covered her head. The Dead Things crept back, delighted to have trapped the Moon. All night they squabbled about how to kill her, until they grew anxious that morning was near and thrust her into the water beneath a heavy stone.

The days passed. Everyone looked forward to the coming of the Moon, but she did not appear. The dark nights remained and the Horrors howled outside people's doors. Families sat up by their fires, fearing that the Things would come for them if the lights went out. Even the Wise Woman, who looked in her book, her mirror and her pot, could not tell them where the Moon had gone.

After many terrible nights, a man from the far fen recalled the time he was saved from death by a dazzling light. Together with his friends, he returned to the Wise Woman. She told them to seek a coffin, a cross and a candle. With stones in their mouths to prevent frightened speech, they set off in the darkness to search for the Moon.

They saw nothing as they edged their way across the quagmire. Slimy hands seemed to pluck at them, sly whispers surrounded them. Much later, quaking with terror, the men saw a long coffin-shaped stone, almost drowned by water. A forked branch stood like a cross, while a will-o'-the-wisp flickered nearby. The searchers prayed from the bottom of their hearts as they heaved at the stone. For an instant they saw a strange, beautiful face looking up at them; then they stepped away from the light. At once all the Horrors fled wailing back to their holes. The next moment, the full Moon shone down from the heavens, revealing the path before them.

Ever since that night, the Moon has shone her brightest over these marshes. Now she knows the Evil Things that lurk there, and she remembers how the men of the fens went out to find her when she was dead and buried.

Question box

When was it safe to cross the fens?
How had the traveller been tricked?
Why did the Dead Things not kill the Moon?
How did the rescuers make sure they would not chatter?
How did the Moon thank the men of the fens?

How did the Moon disguise herself?
What Horrors lived in the marshlands?
Where does the Moon show that she is not selfish?
How did life become unpleasant when the Moon did not appear?
In what way did the Wise Woman's predictions come true?

Exploring ideas

1 **Just fancy that!**

   Imagine how people in the village would have been puzzled when the Moon did not appear as expected. Many people would have tried to explain the mystery.

   Choose one of these characters and write down the explanation he/she gave.

   a) The local Know-All . . . . . who has a scientific explanation for everything.
   b) The village priest . . . . . who has a religious explanation for everything.
   c) A very imaginative child . . . . . who finds the situation an exciting change.

2 Here comes the Bogeyman . . . . .

In the story, the villagers were genuinely terrified of the Dead Things and Nightmare Horrors that were there, outside the door.

If you were a villager, with a particularly troublesome child, and you wanted to make sure that this child would never dare go out at night, what are the stories that you would tell about:

what the Things and Horrors looked like;

what they might do to little children.

3 Speechless

The villagers put pebbles in their mouths to stop them from talking if they were afraid. This might not be the method you would have chosen.

Here is a list of possible ways of keeping quiet. Copy it out as a chart, filling in what you think are the advantages and disadvantages of each method.

Method	Advantages	Disadvantages
Pebbles in the mouth	Easily available/ Cannot be eaten	Grind on your teeth/ Might make you choke
Gag in mouth		
Bag over head		
Suck a dummy		
Sticking plaster over lips		
Hold your tongue		
Smoke a pipe		
Fill mouth with cotton wool		
Suck a large sweet		
Glue lips together		

Can you suggest any other techniques?

4 Private eye

A friend of yours has disappeared. The police are getting nowhere, so you offer to help.

Searching through your friend's home, you spot three significant clues that have been overlooked. These set you off on a trail which eventually leads you to find 'the missing person' unharmed.

The Chief Constable asks you to write a detailed report of how you did it. Be sure to reveal every step you took in tracing your friend and solving the mystery.

5 Lights out!

Radio News bulletins aim to make people listen and understand what has happened.

If, one night, the lights went out in any of the following places, this would be mentioned in a news bulletin.

a) In a lighthouse b) At a busy airport
c) On the main streets of a city

A Radio News producer has given you the task of writing the report on just one of the 'blackout' situations above. Make notes on what could have happened:–

Where? When? Why? Who was involved?
What effect did it have? What was the outcome?

Build these notes up into a News Report for the radio.

6 Small comfort

A FABLE is a simple story where what happens to *animals* often reminds us of how *humans* behave. In these stories the animals are able to talk to each other, like humans.

The most powerful animals do not always come out best at the end. The weaker creature may be cleverer, or more determined.

Think of your own fable, in which a *small* animal is the 'hero'. Remember that your fable should end with a *moral*. This is a sentence in which you make clear what we can learn from the example of these animals.

Discovering words

Learn the language

Here is a detailed account of the rescue of the Moon, as told by one of the people of the fens:

'Well, we all put pebbles in our mouths then we could not scream and the fiends might chase us. We thought we would be lucky to return alive, then we agreed we had to do our best. None of us had ever seen a real live demon and we all knew they were out there in the dark, then we were all shivering and we crept along. We heard awful noises then we felt we were being watched and edged, inch by inch, across the frightful fen, and the terrible fiends just had to be waiting to pounce on us and we were such a clumsy bunch bumping into each other! We were somewhere near the middle of that foul fen, then I decided it would have been much wiser to stay at home, and that night had already given me the nastiest moments of my life. I could hardly bear to think what could happen next, then suddenly a forked branch like a cross was there ahead of us!'

There are far too many '*and*'s and '*then*'s in this story. Other words can join sentences together just as well or better. Here are a few of them:

although	but	since	when
as	for	so	whenever
because	if	until	while

Replace the '*and*'s and '*then*'s with other joining words from the columns above.

Watch your step

The moon appears in a lot of strange places! Each of the following 'moon-words' has been given three meanings. Which one is true?

1 If you saw someone only *once in a blue moon*, you would:
 a) only see the best in them
 b) rarely see them
 c) meet them in your dreams

60

2. A *moonbeam* is:
   a) a ray of light
   b) a scientific weight
   c) an unexpected joke

3. A *mooncalf* is a person who:
   a) never worries
   b) dresses strangely
   c) was born a fool

4. A *moonlight flit* is when someone:
   a) enjoys an outdoor party
   b) chases moths in the dark
   c) moves house to avoid paying bills

5. A *moonflower* is:
   a) an arum lily
   b) an ox-eye daisy
   c) a white narcissus

6. A *moonshiner* earns his living by:
   a) singing romantic ballads
   b) making illegal alcohol
   c) boxing against all challengers

7. If you see a *moonraker* you have come across:
   a) an unexpected meteor
   b) a travelling preacher
   c) a sail on the horizon

8. A person who is *moonstruck* suffers from:
   a) bad eyesight
   b) confusion of the mind
   c) a stiff neck

9. Someone who talks a lot of *moonshine* is full of:
   a) fanciful schemes
   b) false compliments
   c) ridiculous prejudices

10. A person who is a *moonlighter* works:
    a) fixing street lights
    b) when he does not have to pay tax
    c) on weather reports

Make a stop

A book title usually has a capital letter to begin the first word and other important words. Write these titles out with capital letters and put each title in single quotation marks.

living legends of leicestershire

how to be a champion pig breeder

a collection of sea shanties together with sailors' yarns and other maritime memories

ghosts and goblins of fenland

proposed schemes for dyke and ditch drainage across the fens

a hundred and one uses for fresh horse manure

local superstitions recalled by several sober citizens of lincoln

old lancashire medicinal remedies

The path across the marsh quizword

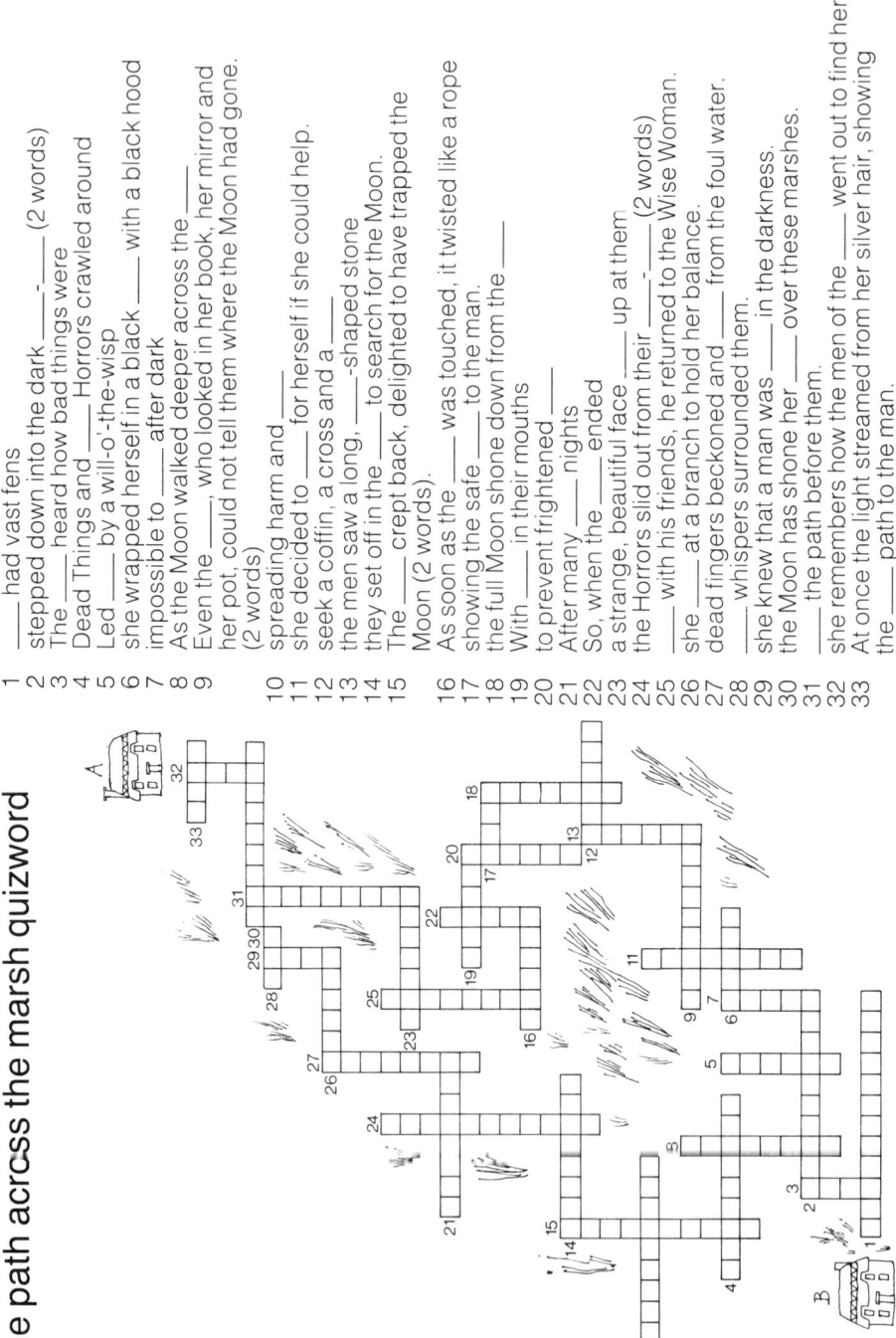

1. ___ had vast fens
2. ___ stepped down into the dark ___-___ (2 words)
3. The ___ heard how bad things were
4. Dead Things and ___ Horrors crawled around
5. Led ___ by a will-o'-the-wisp
6. she wrapped herself in a black ___ with a black hood
7. impossible to ___ after dark
8. As the Moon walked deeper across the ___
9. Even the ___, who looked in her book, her mirror and her pot, could not tell them where the Moon had gone. (2 words)
10. spreading harm and ___
11. she decided to ___ for herself if she could help.
12. seek a coffin, a cross and a ___
13. the men saw a long, ___-shaped stone
14. they set off in the ___ to search for the Moon.
15. The ___ crept back, delighted to have trapped the Moon (2 words).
16. As soon as the ___ was touched, it twisted like a rope
17. showing the safe ___ to the man.
18. the full Moon shone down from the ___
19. With ___ in their mouths
20. to prevent frightened ___
21. After many ___ nights
22. So, when the ___ ended
23. a strange, beautiful face ___ up at them
24. the Horrors slid out from their ___-___ (2 words)
25. with his friends, he returned to the Wise Woman.
26. she ___ at a branch to hold her balance.
27. dead fingers beckoned and ___ from the foul water.
28. ___ whispers surrounded them.
29. she knew that a man was ___ in the darkness.
30. the Moon has shone her ___ over these marshes.
31. ___ the path before them.
32. she remembers how the men of the ___ went out to find her
33. At once the light streamed from her silver hair, showing the ___ path to the man.

The world of the dead moon

This is an English folk story from Lincolnshire. Only a hundred years ago there was no man-made lighting out of doors. The waxing and waning of the moon could mean the difference between life and death.

Who's in it?

The Moon .... a beautiful lady
A man from the far fen
The Wise Woman
Other fen folk
Dead Things and
Nightmare Horrors ..... evil inhabitants of the marsh

What happens?

1 The fens are haunted by Evil Things, so the Moon comes down to try to help the people there.
2 She sinks into the marsh and is trapped.
3 With the light from her hair, she manages to save a lost traveller.
4 The Evil Things imprison her beneath a large stone.
5 The fen folk live in fear because the Moon no longer shines.
6 They consult the Wise Woman who is unable to help them.
7 Finally, the rescued man tells his friends how he was saved by a bright light.
8 The Wise Woman instructs the fen folk as to how the Moon can be found.
9 After a frightening search, they find and release her.
10 In gratitude, the Moon always shines brightly over the fens.

Step into the drama world

The Moon became trapped in a marsh but was rescued by ordinary people.

Step one   Only some paths are safe.
Step two   A trap is unexpected.
Step three   A long argument leads to no decision.
Step four   Co-operation overcomes a challenge.

And it *can* happen now . . . . .

Step one

Stand with your back against one of the walls of the room, not too close to anyone else. You are at the start of a narrow path over a dangerous marsh. You are going to walk ten paces along this path, which has several sharp bends.
Follow *your* path slowly and carefully. (Avoid crossing other people's paths.) When you have walked your ten paces, turn around and come back along *exactly* the same route.
Do this again, making sure that you travel by the identical path, and reach the same spot. Return by the same route.
Imagine that it is now completely dark. Close your eyes. Try to walk the same track as before.

Step two

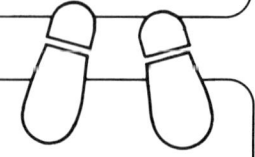

Find a partner. Stand facing each other

You are going to shake hands, in a pleasant relaxed way, only to find that you are unable to let go. Your hands have stuck!
It may seem funny at first, but gradually your efforts to escape will become more serious.

Finally, you will both have to give up and lie down 'exhausted'. Your hands are still stuck.
(You are working *together* to try to escape and must be careful not to hurt your partner.)
Now plan a meeting between two strangers, where the handshake goes wrong in the same way. Decide what they would *think* of each other, and *say* to each other.

Step three

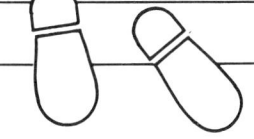

Groups of three

One of the group receives a telephone call. They are being offered a free holiday together, if they can all agree *quickly* on where to go. Everyone is delighted, but they all have their own ideas where the holiday should be. No one will accept anyone else's opinion.
The caller rings back. The same person answers and has to admit that they have not yet agreed. Their chance of a free holiday has been lost!

Step four

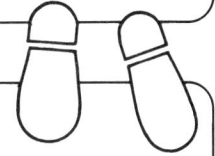

Groups of four/five, A, B, C, D, (E)

You have been instructed to break into a safe in a top-security building at night-time. Your aim is to photograph an important document. You will only succeed if everyone plays their part and co-operates. Each member of the team has a specific task:
A must make sure that the mission takes no longer than three minutes.
B must remember the position and direction of all the burglar alarms.
C must remember the combination for the dial on the safe.
D must remember the reference number of the special document.
E (or D) must photograph the document.
The teacher will tell B, C, and D the *exact* details they have to remember.
Is your mission a success? Act it!

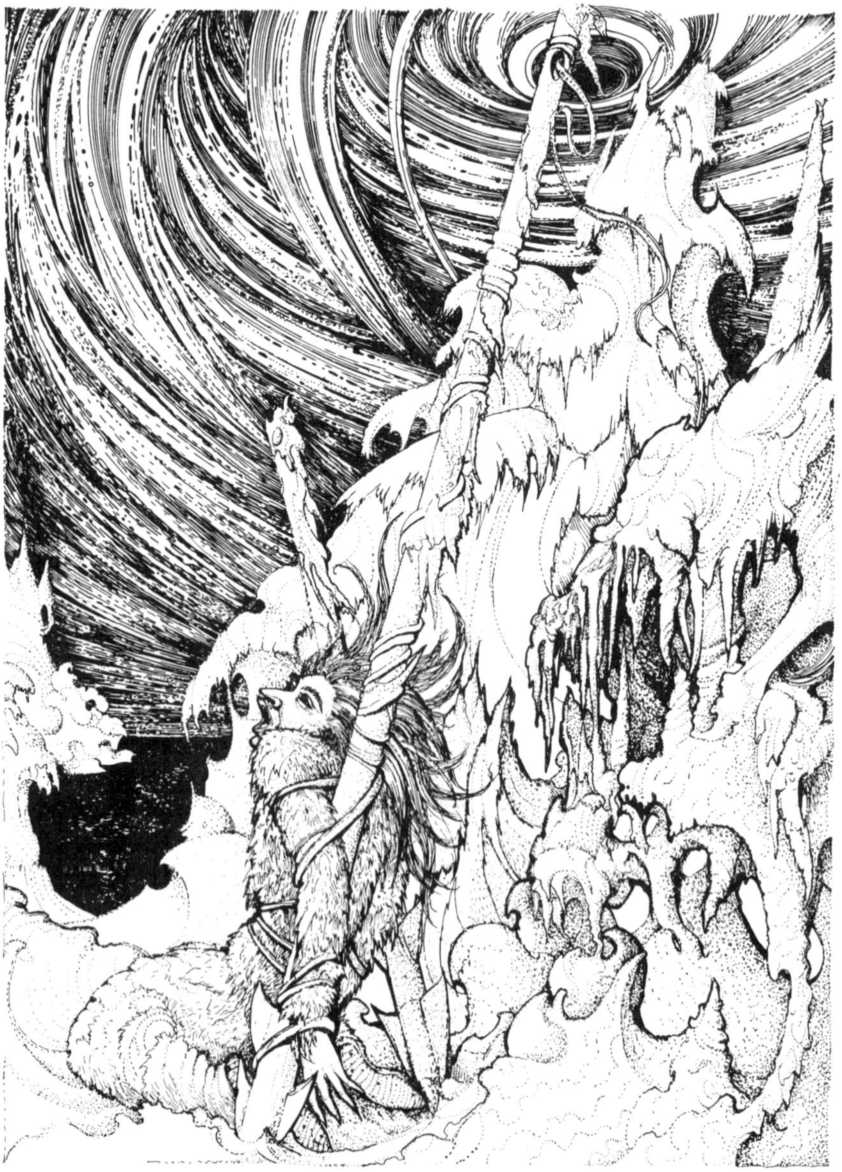

6 The world of rivalry

The Final Victory

Even before our grandfathers were born, there lived two hunters, Tuk and Nahnuk, who were great rivals. If Tuk caught a seal, Nahnuk would chase a faster one. Should Nahnuk slay a white bear and bring home its pelt, before long Tuk would lay a finer fur upon his bed. Other folk in the village laughed at the ways of Tuk and Nahnuk, yet these two would risk their lives to trap any creature that the other could not match.

One day, the two hunters set out in their kayaks to snare the big fish due at that cold time of year. The fishing ground was not a wide one, and soon they floated close together, shouting their boasts of the catches they would make. After a while the wind grew wild. Needing all their skills to keep their kayaks afloat, Tuk and Nahnuk lost sight of the landmarks that guided them.

Some time later, the wind dropped in strength and the two hunters saw an island. Though completely lost, they were so tired that they dragged their kayaks onto the shore. Neither spoke, each secretly blaming the other for their misfortunes.

Suddenly they heard noisy squeals nearby. Nahnuk crept cautiously round a bank of snow to see what was happening. There, before his eyes, he was amazed to find a group of three dwarfs laughing and joking together. He crouched down and threw himself forward, grabbing the smallest dwarf in his fingers. The other two screamed at this attack, but vanished down holes close by. The captured dwarf bit and scratched, frantic to escape, but Nahnuk held it tightly. Grinning triumphantly, he returned to Tuk, waving his trophy: a wriggling, squealing dwarf. Nahnuk claimed that he had made his greatest capture, and that his rival could *never* equal it.

Tuk warned that it should be set free at once, because all dwarfs were protected by the fierce Wind-gods. But Nahnuk refused to release the proof that he was the better hunter.

As night fell, the winds began to bite. The two hunters could not leave the island at this hour and so they prepared to stay. They built small shelters with skins and spears from their kayaks. These should have kept them warm, but the wind howled and stalked around their tents like a monstrous bear.

Inside their flimsy shelters, neither Tuk nor Nahnuk could sleep. The dwarf, which Nahnuk had lashed with a thong to a harpoon driven into the ground, screamed and cursed as it tried to summon the Wind-god to its rescue. Angrily, Nahnuk knocked the little man to the ground and swore at it to hold its tongue. In his tent, Tuk could hear the terrible screams which the wind seemed to echo.

Suddenly, Tuk thought he heard a hissing voice, apparently carried on the wind. Faint but clear, it seemed to say again and again: 'Pour water on your house! Pour water on your house!' Tuk was frightened by this strange message, but he knew that the cold wind could kill him. Hugging his furs around him, Tuk stumbled from the shelter down to his kayak where he kept large seal-skin pouches. These he scooped into the dark water of the sea. Almost blown off his feet, he reeled back to pour the water over his tent. Still the wind howled its message, and Tuk continued to drench the tent with sea-water until the words faded away. Exhausted, he slumped into his shelter and soon, despite the distant screams, fell asleep.

The next morning, when Tuk awoke, he found that he was warm inside an ice-house, the first igloo. The wind had saved him by changing the water into ice. Tuk hacked his way out and immediately saw Nahnuk's spears and skins collapsed over his frozen body. The thong that had tied the dwarf had been chewed through. Not only was the dwarf gone, it had taken Nahnuk's spirit with it as a prisoner.

Question box

Which creatures did the two Eskimos hunt?
Where were the homes of the dwarfs?
What equipment did the hunters take with them in their kayaks?
Why was Tuk still alive in the morning?
What was the dwarf's revenge?

When do the Wind-gods prove their power?
Where does Nahnuk show his nasty side?
Why did Nahnuk not soak his tent like Tuk did?
How did the dwarf escape?
What does this story warn you against?

Exploring ideas

1 **We regret to announce . . . . .**

When someone well-known dies, a newspaper may want to publish an obituary. An obituary should say the good things about the person's life and character, making their death sound like a sad loss.

Imagine that you are asked by the *Arctic Times* to write an obituary for Nahnuk. Begin: 'We regret to announce the death of a popular local figure, Nahnuk the hunter . . . . .'

Make up any details you like to do with Nahnuk's life.

2 A day in the life of an Eskimo dwarf

We know very little about the way Eskimo dwarfs live. All the story really tells us is that they laugh, and joke, and live down holes!

Write as though you are a dwarf describing a day in your life. Details you could include are:

    what your home is like

    what you wear and eat

    what you are afraid of

    any work you do

    how you entertain yourselves

    family life

    your friends and neighbours

3 Do-it-yourself

In order to survive, Tuk and Nahnuk had to make tents. The ground was hard with ice, and their only materials were skins, spear and thongs.

Imagine that you are contributing to a 'Survival Kit for Eskimos' which contains details of how to make the best of things, in bad conditions. Give, stage by stage, clear instructions on how to construct a shelter, using only skins, spears and thongs. It will help to number each step. It may be useful to provide a diagram to illustrate your directions.

4 Curse him!

'The dwarf screamed and cursed as it tried to summon the Wind-god to its rescue.' The furious dwarf was calling the Wind-god to make terrible things happen to Nahnuk.

It might have begged: 'O Mighty Wind-god, protector of all dwarfs, drive chills and aches into every bone of this wicked man's body!'

Think of as many more 'curses' as you can that would make Nahnuk's life miserable with different punishments. Write them down, remembering that they should sound terrifying if read aloud!

5 Tooth and claw

In the story, the wind is described as though it were a vicious animal. This makes it seem all the more powerful and frightening. 'The wind howled and stalked around their tents like a monstrous bear.' 'A hissing voice . . . . .'

Describe in an 'animal-way':

either A fire raging out of control

or A flooded river bursting its banks

When Tuk was in his kayak at the mercy of the wind and waves, it must have seemed as though he was having to fight off **two** wild animals to stay alive. Imagine how he could later describe this perilous struggle, comparing the sea and the storm to savage creatures.

Think of details to include that should send shivers down any spine. . . . .

Then write Tuk's description of *A Storm at Sea*.

6 Winner takes all?

Think back to a time when you were actually taking part in some activity where there had to be a loser as well as a winner. Try and remember everything that made the occasion so important to you, such as: who else was involved/why you were taking part/how much it meant to you/what were your chances of winning.

Write down carefully what happened. Capture as much of the feeling of excitement as you possibly can.

Do not reveal whether you were a winner or a loser until the very last sentence!

Discovering words

Learn the language

Everything has a name. A 'name-word' is called a **noun**. When there is more than one of the thing, we write it in the **plural**. Often this means adding only an s to the noun.

So, for example:
- hunter .... hunters   wind .... winds
- kayak .... kayaks   igloo .... igloos

Some nouns need to add **es** to make them plural:
- volcano .... volcanoes   tomato .... tomatoes

There are other special plurals that you have to learn.

a) Find and write the plurals of these nouns from the story:
- life .... ?   tooth .... ?   foot .... ?
- dwarf .... ?   man .... ?   body .... ?
- trophy .... ?   tongue .... ?
- proof .... ?   pouch .... ?

b) Now write the plurals of these other nouns. Your dictionary may help you, because some of them are unusual.

potato	mouse	success	misery	memory
wife	loss	wolf	hero	branch
sheep	child	tragedy	goose	journey
chief	woman	knife	deer	thief

c) Are any of these plurals made in the same patterns?
List plural words from above that have the same pattern like memor**ies**, miser**ies** and hero**es**, potato**es**

Make a stop

Here is an example of Tuk and Nahnuk discussing their latest captures.

'What have you got there, Nahnuk?'

'None of your business!'

'It's a bear-skin, isn't it?'

'A bigger one than you'll ever catch!'

The two most simple rules for writing down conversations are:

All words that were actually spoken must have speech marks, called inverted commas '. . . . .' at the beginning and end. This book uses single inverted commas. When you write you can use double inverted commas ". . . . ."

When there is a change of speaker there should be a change of line.

a) Try and set out, in a clear way, this argument between Tuk and Nahnuk. Work out *who* says *what*.

Look what I've got! What is it? A dwarf, of course! Let it go, Nahnuk. It is dangerous! What do you mean? I won't let it bite me. No, I don't mean that! The Wind-gods protect dwarfs. What a load of rubbish! Don't think you'll beat me that easily, Tuk.

b) Imagine how this argument could have continued. Write it.

Watch your step

Some groups of words can be especially tricky to read aloud. Your tongue seems to trip over them and so they are called tongue-twisters.

One sentence from the story is: 'After a while the wind grew wild.' Try and say this quickly several times. It is easy to get muddled or stuck.

Here are some more tongue-twisters:

The clumsy kitchen clock click-clicked.
Three grey geese on the green grass grazing.
Six sieves of sifted thistles and six thistle sifters.
The sixth sheik's sixth sheep's sick.
Peggy Babcock.

Try saying each one four times each.

Do you know any more tongue-twisters? Write them down and try to make up some new ones.

The igloo quizword

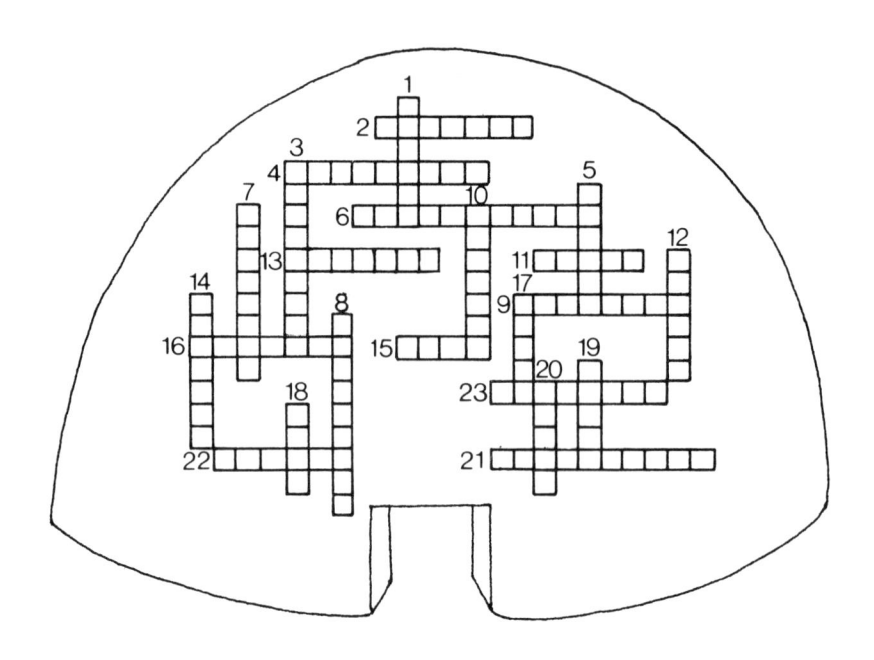

Find the words from the story.

1. two hunters, Tuk and Nahnuk, who were great ___
2. The ___ ground was not a wide one.
3. & 4. Tuk and Nahnuk ___ (2 words) of the ___ that guided them.
5. the two hunters saw an ___
6. Neither spoke, each secretly blaming the other for their ___
7. The ___ dwarf bit and scratched, frantic to escape
8. & 9. all dwarfs were ___ by the fierce ___-___ (2 words)
10. Nahnuk ___ to release the proof that he was the better hunter.
11. The ___, which Nahnuk had lashed with a thong to a harpoon
12. it tried to summon the Wind-god to its
13. In his tent Tuk could hear the terrible ___
14. Tuk was frightened by this strange ___
15. he knew that the ___ wind could kill him.
16. Tuk stumbled from the ___ down to his kayak
17. he reeled back to pour the ___ over his tent.
18. The next morning, when Tuk awoke, he found that he was ___
19. & 20. inside an ice-___, the first ___
21. Tuk hacked his way out and immediately saw Nahnuk's spears and skins collapsed over his ___ (2 words)
22. & 23. it had taken Nahnuk's ___ with it as a ___

The world of Tuk and Nahnuk

This story comes from the Inuit (Eskimo) people of the Arctic. In this harsh world, survival was always precarious and the sea more than the land provided the bulk of food. Creatures like the seal were essential for diet and warmth. The Inuit believed that any offence against the power of the gods would result in swift destruction.

Who's in it?

Tuk ....a hunter
Nahnuk.............another hunter, his rival
Three dwarfs ....
Wind-gods ....guardians of the dwarfs

What happens?

1. Tuk and Nahnuk, rival hunters, set out to catch fish.
2. During a storm at sea they lose their way in their kayaks.
3. They land on an unknown island which turns out to be the home of dwarfs.
4. Nahnuk traps a dwarf and feels very pleased with himself.
5. Tuk advises him to set the dwarf free to avoid the anger of the Wind-gods.
6. Nahnuk refuses and ties up the dwarf for the night.
7. The hunters build tents against the freezing winds.
8. A voice in the wind tells Tuk to pour water on his tent.
9. The winds turn the tent into a warm ice-house.
10. In the morning Tuk finds the dwarf gone, and Nahnuk dead.

Step into the drama world

Tuk and Nahnuk were rivals, and this led to a tragic conclusion.

Step one   They were always keen to compete with each other.
Step two   When they got lost, they each believed it was the other's fault.
Step three One of them under-estimated the power of a stranger.
Step four The other one survived the cold, thanks to a clever idea.

And it *can* happen now . . . . .

Step one

Stand in pairs, facing each other

Cover your knee-caps with your hands.
You are aiming to hit your rival's knee-caps but not let him strike yours.
A point is scored by either competitor when their *hand* hits the *front* of their opponent's knee-cap.
Each time a 'score' takes place, shake hands with your rival.
'Knee-box' for two minutes.
Who wins?

Step two

Find a partner A and B

You are on a country walk together along footpaths.
A is using a map to find the route.
B questions every decision that A makes about the direction they should take.
It starts to rain heavily. They are lost.
Each blames the other.
What happens?

Step three

Groups of three A, B and C

A and B, good friends, meet a stranger, C.
A tries to be polite and friendly with C.
B considers C 'below' him for some reason, and is unpleasant to him.
A tries to get B to show some consideration for C's feelings, but B continues to be ill-mannered.
At some point an important interview is mentioned that B is looking forward to . . . . . and then they realize that C is going to be the interviewer!
What happens?

Step four

Groups of four/five

You are out walking on a deserted moorland on a winter's day. An unexpected blizzard starts, and the temperature falls rapidly. You spot the ruins of a cottage and it seems to be your only hope. You have no means of lighting a fire, so how can you try to keep warm? You will have to be very determined if you are to stand a chance of surviving.
Act it.

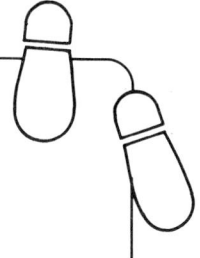

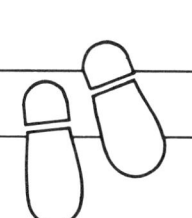

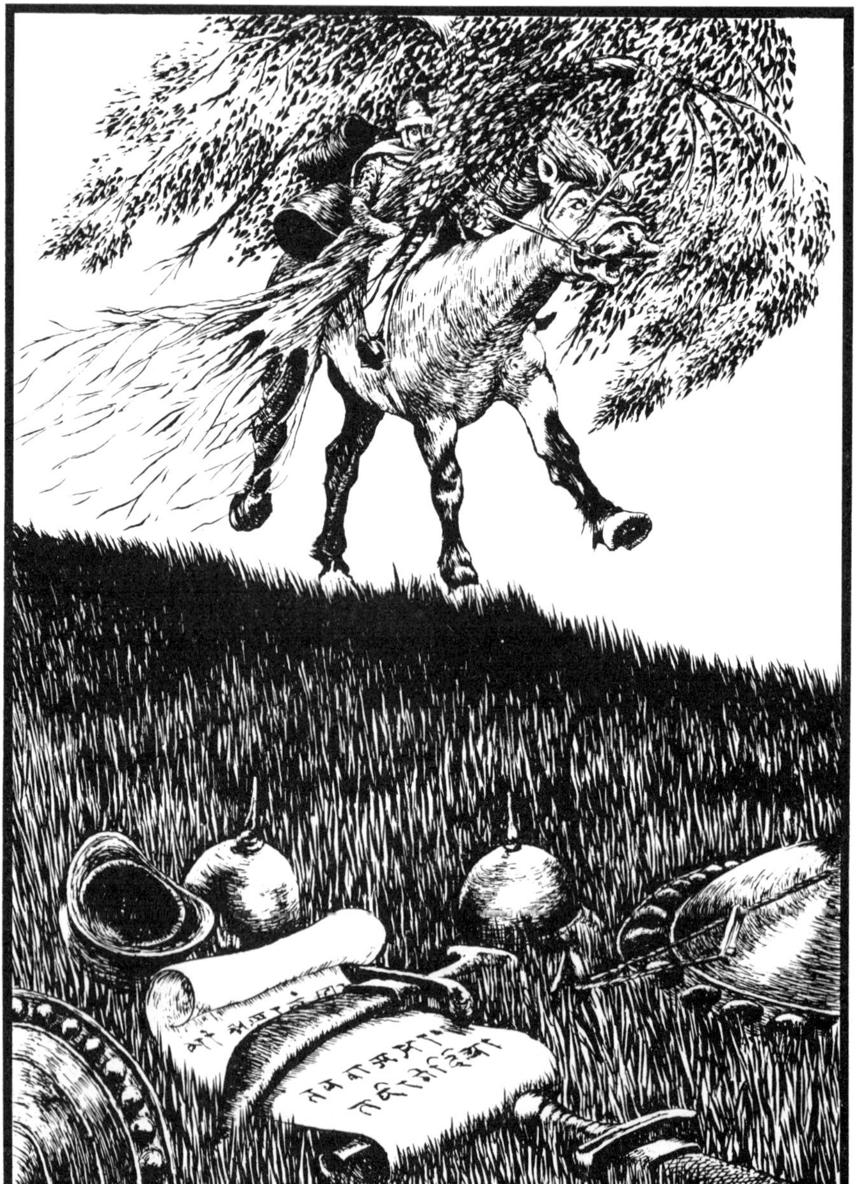

7 The world of surprises

The Man of Many Mistakes

Outside an old woman's tumbledown house, a man-eating tiger was sheltering from the rain. Inside the house, the old woman was grumbling loudly about the storm, saying that the terrible downpour was worse than any tiger. The tiger pricked up its ears at this, and wondered who this 'terrible downpour' was. Just at that moment, a chattee-maker called Ganesh lurched drunkenly along the road, searching for his donkey. He saw the tiger in the shadow near the house and grabbed it by the ear, mistaking it for his lost donkey. Then he started to beat it. The tiger was so terrified by this harsh treatment that it believed Ganesh must be 'the terrible downpour' that the old woman had been talking about. Leaping on the tiger's back, Ganesh then rode it home and tied it to a post.

The next day, his wife discovered the tiger still tied to the post. Ganesh had no idea how the tiger had got there, but the news of the exploit spread through the village and reached the Rajah. The mighty Rajah and his advisers came to marvel at the captured tiger; they were so impressed that Ganesh was made a Lord and a General.

Not long afterwards, a neighbouring ruler prepared to invade the kingdom. The other generals in Ganesh's country refused to fight, and so the Rajah raised Ganesh to the rank of Commander-in-Chief of the Horsemen. Although Ganesh could not even ride a horse, he thanked the Rajah, intending to find a quiet pony for himself. However, the Rajah presented him with a magnificent stallion which Ganesh had to take home to prepare for the battle.

Knowing that her husband was unable to ride, Ganesh's wife hoisted him on to the massive horse and fixed his legs securely with a strap beneath the animal's stomach. The horse was greatly disturbed by this procedure and galloped off out of control, with Ganesh clinging to its mane. Soon Ganesh realized that he was heading towards the enemy camp. This terrified him so much that he decided to grab at a big banyan-tree to bring himself to a stop. He was travelling so fast that the tree was uprooted from the ground into his arms. Instead of stopping him, it made him roar with pain.

The enemy look-outs saw the gigantic horse and what looked like a vast man upon it. Confused messages spread through the camp of the approach of an army of mighty warriors: men who tore up trees in their bellowing rage. These messages grew into horrifying rumours and soon the entire enemy army was in a state of panic. They compelled their leaders to write a peace-treaty and then they fled as fast as they could.

When Ganesh arrived at the camp, the strap holding him on broke from the strain and at last he fell from the horse. Nobody was there to see him as he moaned about his aches and pains and limped among the tents. He discovered all the riches the enemy had left behind, as well as the treaty of peace. He took the treaty with him as he hobbled away, leading the horse. When he arrived home, he told his wife to send the treaty to the Rajah, together with the horse, so that he would never have to ride the animal again.

The next day Ganesh walked to the palace. After his success in putting all the enemy troops to flight, everybody was amazed that he simply walked up to the palace doors rather than riding there in state. The Rajah was impressed by Ganesh's modesty as well as by his bravery. So he raised him to the highest rank and presented him with all the captured wealth.

Now a rich man, Ganesh lived free, happy and undisturbed. He never forgot the strange workings of Fortune, and, grateful for all these favours, allowed the tiger to return to the jungle, where it lived long and peacefully, telling its tales of 'the terrible downpour'.

Question box

Why was Ganesh out in the rain?
Why did the tiger not attack Ganesh?
What made the horse gallop off?
What did Ganesh's wife send to the Rajah?
How did Ganesh show his gratitude to Fortune?

What is your idea of a 'tumbledown house'?
How do you imagine the Rajah found out about Ganesh's tiger?
Why do you think Ganesh felt he had to ride the stallion?
What frightened the enemy look-outs?
Where does anyone make any *mistakes* in this story?

Exploring ideas

1 Tiger tale

Suppose the tiger told the story from his point of view to the other animals in the jungle.

The tiger would make sure that everyone believed that:
  he stood no chance against an incredibly powerful enemy;
  his final escape was brilliantly planned, and daringly carried out.

Write a really convincing tale.

2 In black and white

Suppose that you are a reporter who has been sent to interview Ganesh's wife and the Rajah. The Rajah will describe Ganesh as a remarkable national hero. Ganesh's wife will be determined to prevent her husband getting involved in any more risky adventures, and will tell what an unreliable and foolish man he really is.

You will receive two totally different impressions of the same person.

Write a brief report of each interview.

3 Excuses, excuses!

The Rajah's generals were unwilling to fight, so they would have had to find excuses for *not* fighting that the Rajah would believe.

Put yourself in their place. To save your job, and your head, you will have to give good reasons.

Not all of these would please the Rajah:

'I think it would be better to play for time................................,'
'A few chaps on the other side are friends of mine ....,'
'We are not prepared for such an attack.................................,'
'It's not in my conditions of service ....,'
'There are more of them than us ....,'
'I'm bound to mess it up..,'
'My feet hurt ....,'
'Our weapons are inferior ....,'
'Actually, I'm visiting a friend this afternoon..........................,'
'There is no suitable battleground for our cavalry....................,'
'It's my rest day..,'
'I'd love to, but isn't it someone else's turn............................?'

Choose the reasons which you think the Rajah might accept, and use these ideas to build up a 'speech of apology'. Write it down.

4 And lived to tell the tale . . . . .

Few people enjoy danger when they are actually facing it, but it can make a good story afterwards.

You might have had a thrilling adventure. If so, you could choose to write about this. If not, imagine *one* of the following situations in which you would be at risk:

a) On a bolting horse
b) Right on the edge of the roof of a high building
c) In an aeroplane which is out of control

Or describe any other dangerous incident that you can imagine, as though it is happening to you.

Write an account which captures the suspense of such an experience. It is not how you got there that is important, it is what you felt and what you saw.

5 That's the way it goes!

Write a short story about a character who is involved in a series of mistakes or misunderstandings, but for whom everything turns out for the best in the end.

6 Just what you're looking for?

Things can be made to sound much better than they actually are. For instance, if Ganesh wanted to sell the horse that the Rajah had given him, because it was vicious, uncontrollable, much too big and expensive to feed, he might write this advertisement:

> **A RARE OPPORTUNITY** to acquire an unforgettable stallion with a character all of its own.
> Its independent spirit will give you moments of excitement you will always remember!
> Its healthy appetite will astound you and your friends.
> Here is a real challenge for the enthusiastic horse-lover.... An animal everyone will talk about for years to come!

Try and think how you could interest people in:

a) A small terraced house. Dark cramped rooms/peeling wallpaper/no bathroom/damp cellar/old-fashioned kitchen/leaking roof/no garden/busy flyover passes front windows.

b) Seaside resort. Sharp pebbled beach/crumbling cliffs/dangerous tides/sharks close to shore/no amusements or entertainments/unfriendly inhabitants/high rainfall.

You must not tell any lies, but you *can* cleverly make the unattractive features of these places sound more appealing. Write your advertisements.

Discovering words

Learn the language

Ganesh was amazed at the richness of everything he saw inside the Rajah's palace. Here is a description:

> The great door was *yellow* with *red* stars all over it. The wonderful marble staircase was like a *blue* and *green* cascade, while the huge pillars were *red* with *red* streaks. On the *green* walls hung beautiful *blue* and *yellow* tapestries of silk damask. Above the Rajah's *yellow* throne was draped a splendid *red* canopy with *blue* threads woven into it. The *green* cushions, on which he rested his *red* satin slippers, were trimmed with a design of *blue* and *yellow* elephants. His *green* robe was decorated with *red* and *blue* patterns, and he wore a *green* turban on his head. Attendants, in uniforms of *yellow* and *blue*, knelt on either side of him upon a magnificent carpet of *green* and *yellow* birds.

This account would be more interesting if different words were used to describe the colours.

These are some suggestions:

Blues	Greens	Reds	Yellows
azure-blue	apple-green	blood-red	amber-yellow
cobalt-blue	emerald-green	cherry-red	chrome-yellow
ice-blue	lime-green	flame-red	citron-yellow
sapphire-blue	olive-green	rose-red	saffron-yellow
sky-blue	sea-green	ruby-red	sulphur-yellow
turquoise-blue	willow-green	wine-red	topaz-yellow

Find out as much as you can about these colours from your dictionary. Then rewrite the account, using these words, to make it even more colourful.

These describing words are called **adjectives**. Look back to page 24 for more adjectives.

Make a stop

The army of the Rajah can be written more briefly as *The Rajah's army*

To show that it is the army of the Rajah, as well as putting the word Rajah first, you also add 's.

This punctuation mark is called an **apostrophe**.

The word that you put first may already end in an **s**. In this case the apostrophe is added after the **s**.

For example: *The homes of the villagers* would be written as *The villagers' homes*.

Turn these phrases round like the example. Write them out more briefly using apostrophes.

The tents of the army	The flag of a general
The neighing of the horses	The rattle of the wagons
The smoke of a camp fire	The laughter of soldiers
The faces of the look-outs	The sparkle of the armour
The echo of drums	The swords of the bodyguards

Watch your step

Their is written when it means 'belonging to them'.

There is used if the word could be replaced by *here* and still make sense.

Write out this account again, deciding whether each gap needs *their* or *there*.

'We knew that ——— army was over ———. ——— was no chance that ——— soldiers could be far away as ——— was the sound of ——— drums, and we could see the smoke from ——— fires. ——— generals would be ——— too, planning how ——— attack from the hills right back ——— could succeed. Then, all of a sudden, ——— appeared ——— great champion, who rode up ——— on the largest horse from ——— country. ——— was a fearful shout when we saw him ———. In his rage, he had uprooted one of ——— strange trees, and now he roared when he saw us ———. Men started to run away, throwing down ——— weapons, and soon ——— was a wild retreat. Our leaders scribbled a plea for peace with ——— trembling hands, and leapt onto ——— horses. We did not stop running until ——— was no chance that ——— giant warrior could catch us!'

The tiger quizword

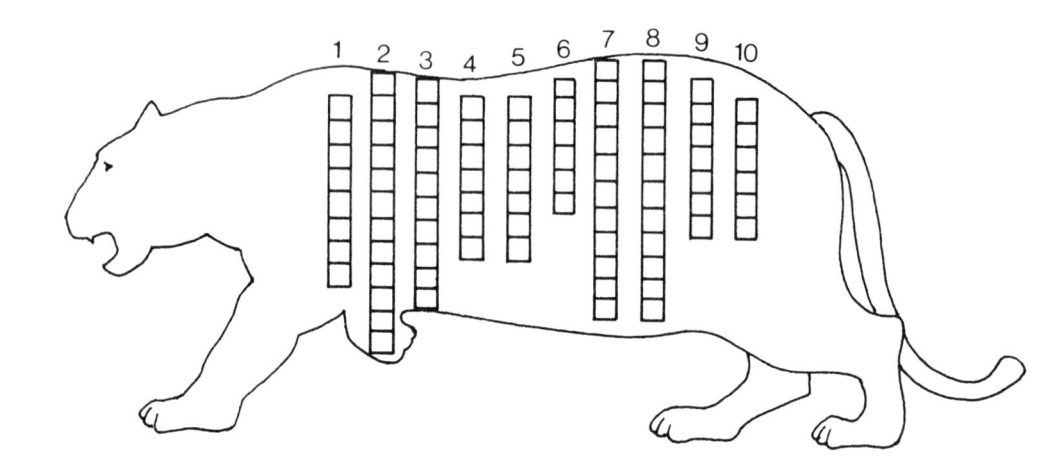

Find the words from the story.

1. the terrible ___ was worse than any tiger.
2. a ___ called Ganesh (2 words)
3. mistaking it for his ___ (2 words)
4. the news of the ___ spread through the village
5. Ganesh was made a Lord and a ___
6. he decided to grab at a big ___ tree
7. They compelled their leaders to write a ___ (2 words)
8. So he raised him to the ___ (2 words)
9. He never forgot the strange workings of ___
10. Ganesh allowed the tiger to return to the ___

The world of Ganesh

This story from the Deccan in central India is set in a time when the land was divided into kingdoms ruled by rich and powerful Rajahs. A poor man needed good luck if he was to become prosperous.

Who's in it?

Ganesh	a maker of chattees (pots)
Mrs Ganesh	his wife
The Rajah	the ruler of the kingdom
Generals	leaders of the Rajah's army
A rival Rajah	the king of a neighbouring country
Enemy soldiers and lookouts	
Tiger	a vicious man-eater
A horse	a high-spirited stallion

What happens?

1. A fierce tiger hears talk of a terrifying creature.
2. Ganesh, who is drunk, mistakes the tiger for his donkey.
3. He drags the tiger home and ties it to a post.
4. Rumours of Ganesh's bravery reach the Rajah.
5. Ganesh is made Commander-in-Chief against enemy invaders and is given a horse.
6. His wife straps Ganesh onto his horse.
7. The horse bolts and Ganesh uproots a tree while attempting to stop.
8. The opposing army flees at the sight of this daunting rider.
9. Ganesh finds a peace treaty in one of the deserted tents.
10. He walks to the palace, where he is rewarded by the Rajah.

Step into the drama world

Despite making many mistakes, Ganesh finds that everything turns out right for him in the end.

Step one   Mistakes occur in recognition.
Step two   He is forced to face an uncomfortable prospect.
Step three   A lot of things go wrong for him.
Step four   He is accepted as an expert although he is not.

And it can happen *now* . . . . .

Step one

Stand in a space

Imagine that your name has been changed to that of someone else in the group. **Do not tell anyone**.
You are outside a busy shop, sheltering under an umbrella in the rain. Because you are trying to meet someone, and you only know their name, you must go up to people and ask politely:
'Excuse me, is your name .... ?
(Use the name of somebody else in the group.) If you guess the right name, the person will admit it and shake hands with you.
If you are wrong, they will deny it politely, and move away. You can ask each other only **one** name at any meeting.
Can you discover anyone's 'name'?

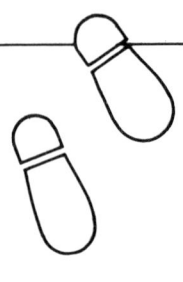

Step two

Pairs . . . parent and child

The child played truant from school yesterday. Now he wants his parents to write a note to cover up for the absence.
The parent is unwilling, and thinks the child should face up to whatever is coming to him! The child is worried and suggests many different excuses his parent could write.
The parent always has reasons, or answers, for not being prepared to give any of these excuses. Can the child think of anything that the parent *will* agree to write?

Step three

Groups of three A, B and C

A is a dissatisfied customer at a shop owned by B.
C is the inefficient employee who has made a bad blunder that causes A to complain strongly to B.
When C is called in, he makes excuses, which B tries to use to prove that the complaint is unfair.
This will not please A. What happens?

Step four

Groups of four or five

Choose someone to be X.
Through rumour, X has gained a reputation. He is supposed to have some ability or talent which he does not really possess! For example, he may be considered 'brainy', 'brave with dangerous animals', 'expert in first aid'.
For the first time a situation has come up where the others expect X to make use of his talent, which they think will be easy for him.
Is he shown up to be a phoney?
Or does he somehow get away with it?

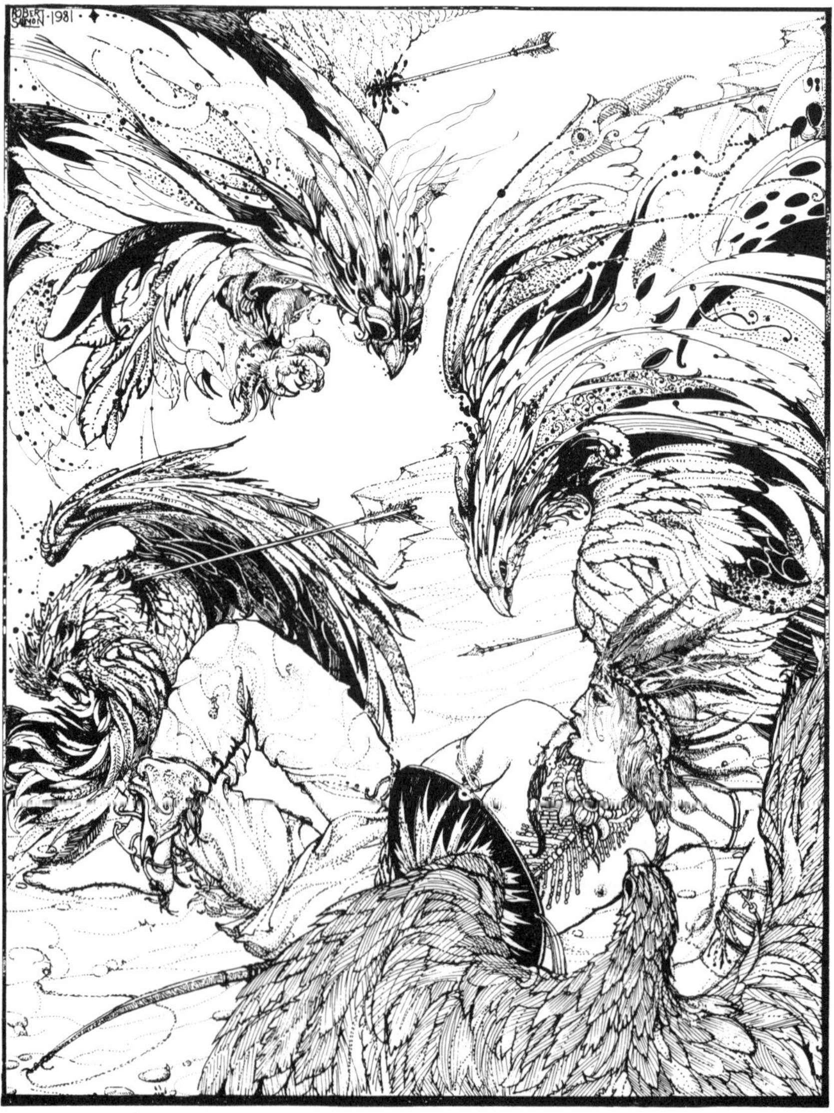
ROBERT
1981

8 The world of courage

The Journey to the Sun

Scar-Face was a fearless brave whose cheek had been ripped by the vicious claw of a grizzly bear he had slain. Many of the old men believed he would do well, but the young braves only jeered at his ugly scar.

The chief of the tribe had a beautiful daughter, called White-Cloud, whom all the young warriors desired in marriage, and Scar-Face had fallen in love with her. One day, although ashamed of his ugliness, he sought White-Cloud by the river, where she was pulling rushes to make baskets. In his quiet yet dignified manner, Scar-Face asked her to dwell with him in his lodge and be his wife. The maiden spoke kindly to him but explained that Sun-God had forbidden her to marry. When Scar-Face said he would seek Sun-God to gain her release from this bond, White-Cloud told him that Sun-God had the power to remove the scar as a sign, should he agree to free her.

For many moons Scar-Face covered the hard trail, crossing rivers and mountains, wide plains and dense forests, but never finding Sun-God's dwelling. He asked the wild creatures that he met, but none knew the right path except, at last, for a wolverine which agreed to guide him. For a long and weary season they travelled together, until they came to a Great Water, too broad and too deep to cross. While Scar-Face sat gloomily on the bank, two black swans floated close to him. They allowed him to sit on their backs and then bore him to the other side. The young warrior thanked the swans, as he had the wolverine, and continued on his way.

Not far ahead, he noticed a bow and arrows on the ground but, because they were not his own, Scar-Face would not touch them. Soon he encountered a handsome youth who enquired if he had seen a bow and arrows. Scar-Face replied that he had passed them shortly before and the boy praised him for his rare honesty, asking if he could help in any way. When the tired brave said that he hoped to reach the home of Sun-God, the boy introduced himself as Morning-Star, child of the Sun.

He led the footsore Indian to a great lodge, glorious with golden light and magnificently decorated. At the entrance stood beautiful Moon-Goddess, mother of Morning-Star, who greeted Scar-Face kindly.

Presently Sun-God himself returned, mighty in his strength like the planet over which he ruled. He too welcomed the brave and invited him to be his guest. After his lonely journey, Scar-Face was glad to stay with such a loving family and hunt with Morning-Star, not wishing to ask his question too hastily. When Sun-God warned them both not to venture near the Great Water because savage birds lurked there, Scar-Face promised him that he would always guard Morning-Star's life with his own.

The two young men hunted long and successfully, but late in the day Morning-Star stole away towards the Great Water, because he was curious about the dangerous birds. Noticing that the boy was gone, Scar-Face followed his tracks until he found him, pinned to the ground by the hideous birds and beating back their ravening beaks with his bow. With no thought for himself, Scar-Face plunged into the fray, slaughtering the awful creatures in his fury.

When they returned to the wonderful lodge, Sun-God gave Scar-Face his heart-felt thanks for the rescue of his beloved son. Then Scar-Face revealed the secret of his love for White-Cloud: the reason for his journey. Sun-God explained that he had chosen this girl for Morning-Star, but now both he and his son would like her to become Scar-Face's bride instead.

With one motion of his bright hand, Sun-God wiped the scar from the warrior's torn cheek. Then the family loaded Scar-Face with many marvellous gifts and showed him a short route back to his own land.

Soon Scar-Face reached home and made his approach to White-Cloud. At first she did not know him, so splendid was his appearance now. But when she recognized him, she ran to his arms with a glad cry, and that same day she became his wife.

Question box

Why did Scar-Face have a scar?
Who was the father of White-Cloud?
What were rushes used for?
How was Sun-God's lodge unusual?
Why did Scar-Face protect Morning-Star?

Why was it the *old* men who thought Scar-Face would do well?
How was Scar-Face's journey difficult?
Where does Scar-Face show the good qualities of his character?
How did Sun-God's family prove they were grateful to Scar-Face?
Why do you think White-Cloud was glad to see Scar-Face?

Exploring ideas

1 A day to remember

All that we are told of the wedding of Scar-Face and White-Cloud is that it took place on the same day as the warrior returned.

Imagine that you are an old Blackfoot story-teller, famous for your tales of days gone by. Although it is several years after the event, you are able to recall what everybody said and did, as though it were yesterday.

Write the story that you could tell the tribe, as they sit around the fire on a cold night.

2 Talk to the animals

On the 'the hard trail, crossing rivers and mountains, wide plains and dense forests', Scar-Face might have met:
buffalo, cougar, coyote, eagle, grizzly bear, rattlesnake, raven, salmon, skunk and stag.

Choose at least five of these animals and, for each one, decide:
a) Where Scar-Face would find it.
b) What it would look like.
c) How it could help him.
d) What compliment he could give it to win its assistance.

You could set your ideas out in a chart, which should fill a whole page, so that you can write a lot about each creature.

Creature	Habitat	Appearance	Help	Compliment

3 The big fight

There are two 'big fights' that are linked to the story. One was against a grizzly bear, the other was against the savage birds.

Write, as if you are Scar-Face, giving a detailed account of what happened on one of these occasions.

4 Only skin-deep

Imagine that *you* once lived with the Blackfoot tribe at the time of Scar-Face. Imagine that you have blond hair, blue eyes and pink skin.

As you do not look like the others in the tribe they might have treated you as either an ugly freak or a beautiful god.

Write your autobiography (the story of your life).

Explain how you came to be in this unusual situation, and what happened in the end.

How did the tribe behave towards you?
What work did they give you to do?
Could you make any real friends?
How did you feel about your life with the tribe?

5 Love will find a way

If you really love somebody, you will take on any challenge to prove how much you care for them. Some real problems that might appear to block 'the path of true love' are:

One person is disabled or disfigured.
The girl is taller/older than the boy.
They live a long way apart.
They come from very different backgrounds.

Write a letter to a magazine describing one of these problems and asking for advice.

Then write a sensible and honest reply.

6 Home sweet home

When Scar-Face reached Sun-God's home, he was 'glad to stay with such a loving family'. It is always very pleasant to spend time in a happy home, but not everyone would agree as to what makes a home 'happy'.

Here are ten suggestions you could consider:

a colour television	plenty of money
brothers and sisters	a modern house
good cooking	good neighbours
a large garden	a loving atmosphere
pets	a telephone

Put these in order of priority (the order you think they are important). Explain in detail why your top three deserve to be top of your list. What else do you think helps to make a happy home?

Discovering words

Learn the language

Here are ten sentences about what different creatures were doing when Scar-Face met them:

1 A golden cougar walked along the steep mountain slopes.
(ambled / prowled / roamed)
2 High in the clear sky the mighty eagles flew.
(glided / hovered / soared)
3 A giant grizzly took a honeycomb from a hollow tree.
(grabbed / plundered / snatched)
4 The bison from the wide plains moved into sight.
(galloped / thundered / trotted)
5 Dozens of gophers dug into the dry desert sands.
(burrowed / delved / tunnelled)
6 Natterjack toads came out of a still pool.
(burst / sprang / vaulted)
7 Far away in the dark starless night a lone coyote called.
(barked / howled / whimpered)
8 Nimble squirrels ran up the tallest trees of the forest.
(clambered / scurried / swarmed)
9 Families of rattlesnakes slept under the warm rocks.
(coiled / dozed / lolled)
10 A beaver bit the logs in its dam across a river.
(chewed / gnawed / nibbled)

Rewrite each sentence replacing the 'action-word' with one from inside the brackets. Choose the word which you think makes the sentence most interesting. Be prepared to explain your choice.

These 'action-words' are called **verbs**. Look back to page 36 for more verbs.

Try a new way

There are many lively old sayings which are called proverbs. They are still in use because they say things which seem to be true. The proverbs below, although they come from England, could certainly fit parts of the Blackfoot story of Scar-Face.

> 'Actions speak louder than words.'
> 'A cat may look at a King.'
> 'Every cloud has a silver lining.'
> 'You can't tell a book by its cover.'
> 'Faint heart never won fair lady.'
> 'A friend in need is a friend indeed.'
> 'Honesty is the best policy.'
> 'Where there's a will there's a way.'
> 'Empty vessels make the most noise.'
> 'Still waters run deep.'

1 Find out what all these proverbs mean.
2 Read through the story again, and see where any of the proverbs seem to be true.
3 Write down those proverbs which you believe fit some part of the story of Scar-Face. Explain *why* you think they fit.

Read the signs

Can you spot what is being described in the following riddles? If you can, write down what you think the answers are and how you worked them out.

1 As I travel my feathers stretch behind me. My head is hard and can part the air, often making me an unwelcome guest.
2 My body is empty and round, as I sit upon the ground, but men beat my skin drawn tight, until my voice cries out for all to hear, yet still their hands pound cruelly.
3 I run so fast that men must pant behind. Never needing to rest, I can neither be trapped or killed, although the people must taste my body or they will die.
4 Shoulder to shoulder, we can hide a warrior from the sun. No brave is mightier than us, and our life is long, but we shake when one of our number is forced to kiss the ground. If we are left alone, many creatures choose to trust our arms.
5 We gather together and whisper to each other, whenever the wind springs up. Our home is where we stand in water reaching up towards the sky. Rough hands tear us from our beds and make us lose our freedom.
6 Invisible though I am, when I bind together those that I visit, they may not escape. At once they are my slaves and stay to serve me. Should I decide to depart a great pain will take my place.

Write some riddles of your own, and see if anyone can solve them.

The Blackfoot quiz-bird

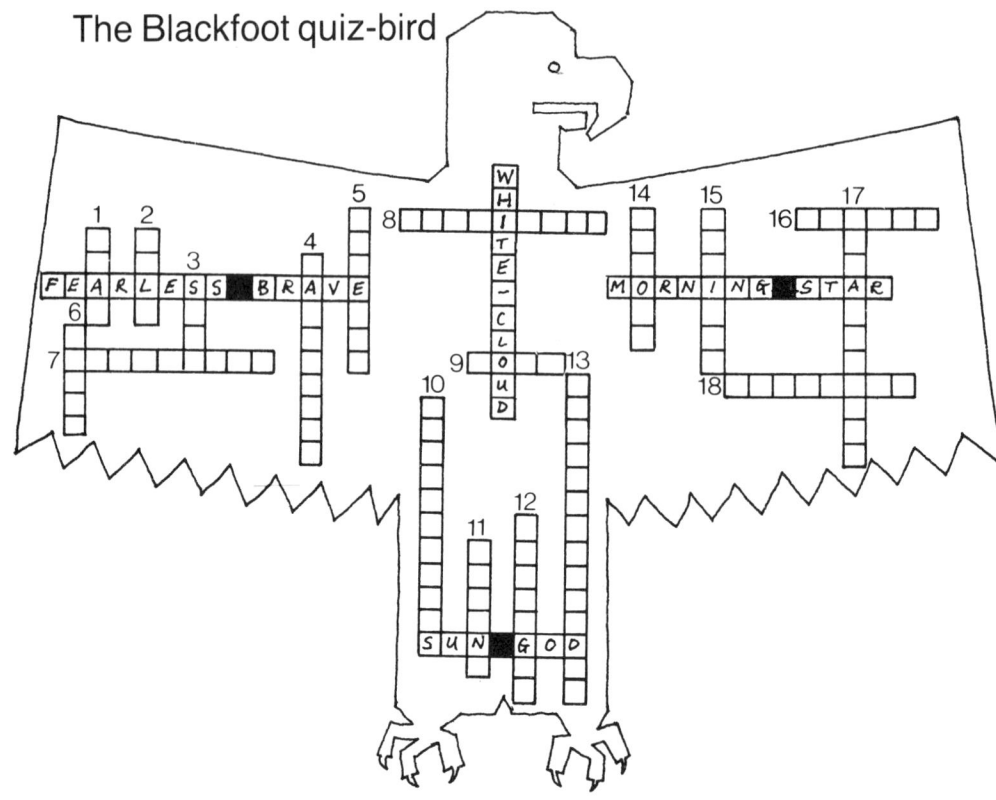

Find the words from the story.

1. the vicious claw of a grizzly ___ he had slain.
2. the young braves only jeered at his ___ scar.
3. Sun-God had the power to remove the ___ as a sign.
4. For many moons Scar-Face covered the ___ (2 words)
5. the boy praised him for his rare ___.
6. two black ___ floated close to him.
7. none knew the right path except, at last, for a ___
8. Sun-God had ___ her to marry.
9. Scar-Face had fallen in ___ with her.
10. At the entrance stood beautiful ___-___ (2 words)
11. Scar-Face was glad to stay with such a ___ family.
12. mighty in his ___ like the planet over which he ruled.
13. When they returned to the ___ (2 words)
14. he noticed a bow and ___ on the ground.
15. Morning-Star stole away towards the Great Water, because he was ___ about the dangerous birds.
16. Sun-God gave Scar-Face his heart-felt thanks for the ___ of his beloved son.
17. not to venture near the Great Water because ___ lurked there. (2 words)
18. beating back their ___ beaks with his bow.

The world of Scar-Face

The Blackfoot Indians of North America believed that every creature had its place in the pattern of existence. They believed too that every brave had to meet the challenges that faced him alone. This story shows how a brave needed integrity, as well as determination.

Who's in it?

Scar-Face	a fearless brave
White-Cloud	a beautiful maiden, daughter of the chief
Morning-Star	a handsome youth
Moon-Goddess	mother of Morning-Star
Sun-God	his mighty father
Members of the tribe	Two black swans
A wolverine	Savage birds

What happens?

1. Scar-Face, a courageous warrior, falls in love with White-Cloud, the daughter of the chief.
2. Sun-God has forbidden her to marry.
3. Scar-Face, determined to win White-Cloud, decides to seek out Sun-God.
4. In his long and difficult journey he is helped by different animals.
5. Because of his honesty, he is aided by Morning-Star.
6. Morning-Star's parents, Sun-God and Moon-Goddess, welcome Scar-Face to their home.
7. While out hunting, Scar-Face saves Morning-Star's life.
8. Sun-God rewards the warrior by freeing White-Cloud to be his bride.
9. The scar is removed and gifts are provided.
10. Scar-Face returns to marry White-Cloud.

Step into the drama world

Scar-Face overcame many difficulties, and was finally rewarded for his courage.

Step one   He made a long and difficult journey.
Step two   He met the one who had the power to grant his wishes.
Step three He risked his own life when disobedience had led somebody into danger.
Step four The others gave him what they valued most highly.

And it *can* happen now . . . . .

Step one

Find a space and stand still

You are going on a difficult journey with *four* different stages. Choose from these: deep sand/thick forests/sharp stones/rushing, shallow streams/long grass/crumbling ledges. Decide what *your* journey will include. You should travel a long way, but it will not be easy or fast. Finally, you will be very tired.
Sit down and rest.

Step two

Get into pairs A and B

A has a serious request to make, and B has the power to grant it. B is **either** an employer who can provide a part-time job.
or a policeman who must agree before an air-gun licence can be given.
or the headmaster who may give permission to the form-representative for an unusual visit.
In all cases, A must give the right impression of being sensible and reliable, giving acceptable answers to any questions B may put. What does B decide?

Step three

Make a group of three, A, B and C

A is B's parent and C is B's friend. The two children ask A's permission to go somewhere. A is not keen to agree because of some danger near where the children wish to go. Permission is granted only after promises have been made to take care.
When B and C get to the place, B does exactly what he has promised *not* to do. It is only through the bravery of C that B's life is saved.
By chance, A arrives on the scene at the end of the rescue. Plan what is going to happen, and be sure to know how the three characters will behave, at the end.
Act it out.

Step four

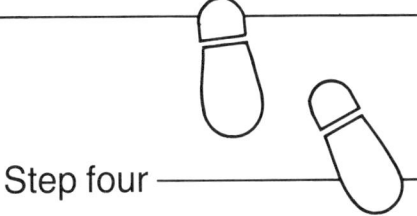

Groups of four or five

A family has a next-door neighbour, (X), who is moving away from the district. X lives alone, and has been very kind and helpful over a number of years, so the family plan a get-together a week before X moves.
During the farewell party it becomes clear that X would like to take the family's much-loved pet to the new home.
Are they prepared to give up the thing they love to make someone else happy? Can they agree?
Try it out.

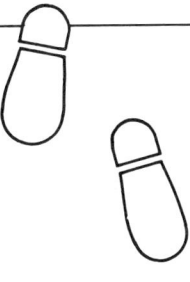

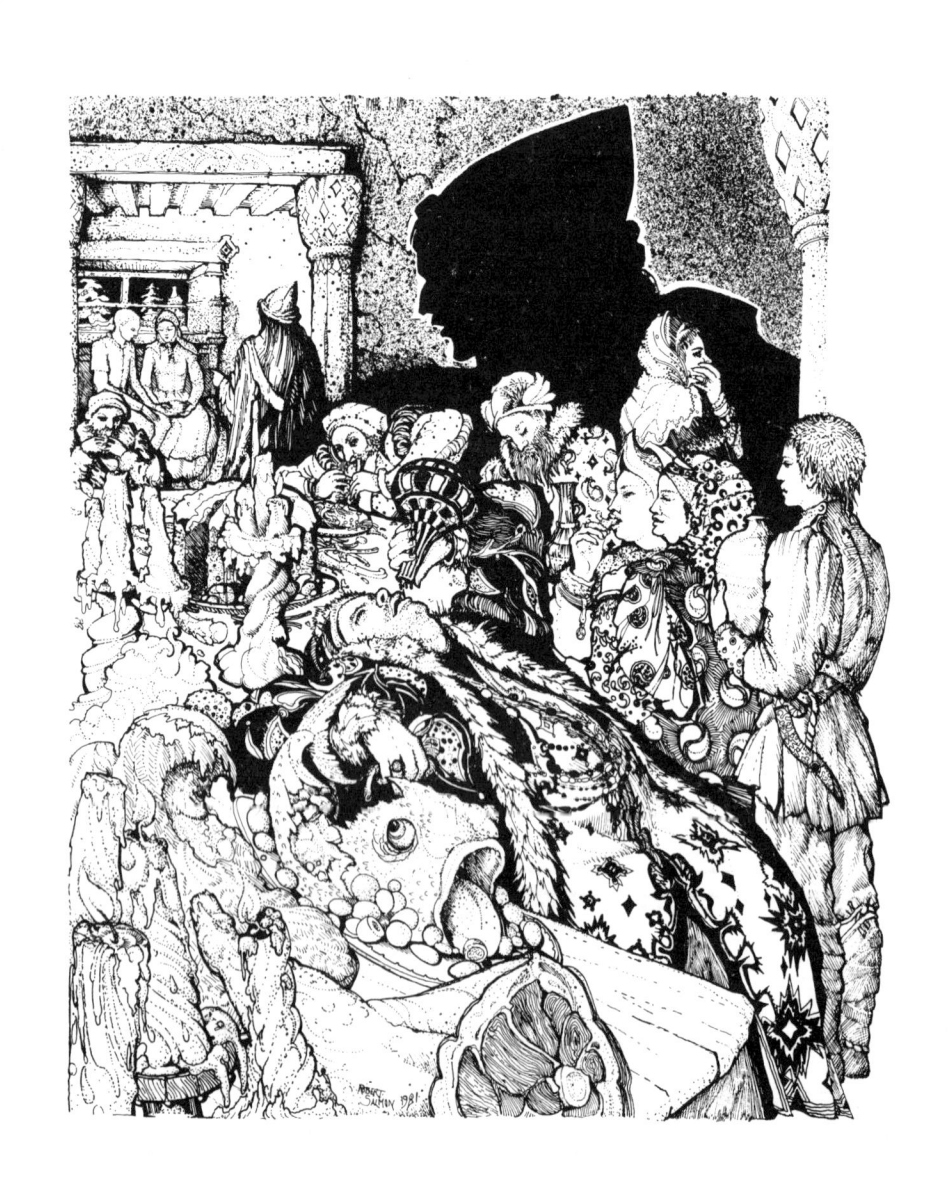

9 The world of despair

The Two Brothers

A long time ago there lived two brothers, Saran and Yumart. Saran was mean and kept all his money, while Yumart found that his generosity made him poor. Soon, Yumart realized he would have to leave his farm to support his family. His brother offered to employ him as a labourer and Yumart had to agree. Saran was delighted to have Yumart under his control for a pitiful wage.

Several months later, Saran wanted to celebrate his birthday and invited all the wealthy, local merchants. In order to show how rich he was, he told Yumart to attend the event with his wife. Unkindly, Saran hoped that their poverty would contrast with his own wordly success. Yumart and his wife prepared for the feast, knowing that they could not avoid this humiliation.

Dressed in tatters, they sat in a shadowy corner of the room and were treated with contempt, given the scraps others did not want. The other guests, who were full of vodka and laughter, began to sing in a hearty manner. Yumart suddenly decided that, as he had been unable to afford a present, he was going to contribute a song to his brother's party. When Yumart's voice rang out, deep and rich, it attracted much attention and praise. Oddly, it seemed to Yumart that he was accompanied by a second voice, one that was flat and dry, coming from a gaunt figure seated on a stool in the shadows nearby. This stranger approached Yumart and introduced himself as Mr Misery. He complained that he had been close to Yumart for many months and that he thought it was about time he was treated as one of the family. Yumart was so taken aback that he did not argue when

Misery announced that he intended to play a far greater part in Yumart's future life.

This turned out to be all too true. Misery led Yumart into foolishness and waste. Soon Yumart was forced to sell his possessions: his wooden sledge, his last chair and his saucepan, to buy kegs of vodka for Misery. When he had drunk the vodka, Misery always became even more miserable and grumbled at Yumart, whose life plunged from bad to worse.

Finally Yumart had nothing left. Misery ranted and raved at him, leapt onto his back and drove him from the house. Deep in the dark forest, Misery pulled him to a halt and jumped to the ground by a round rock, leaving Yumart doubled over, panting with exhaustion. He ordered Yumart to push the rock to the side revealing a dark hole. This held Misery's secret store of roubles, with which he could buy vodka when his 'hosts' had been driven to poverty.

Misery took out several large money-bags and leaned over to push the others out of sight. Sensing a chance to escape, Yumart flung himself desperately at the rock, which crashed back onto the hole and trapped Misery inside. Yumart collected the bags of roubles and returned home, laughing and singing with relief to be rid of his unwelcome guest.

Now Yumart's whole life changed for the better. He no longer needed to work for Saran and could even employ others to plough his fields for him. He had a fine house built for his family, who began to enjoy pleasures they had long forgotten.

Hearing of his brother's new wealth, Saran decided to visit him and learn his secret. All that Yumart would tell him was that the changes in his life had come from beneath a round rock in the forest.

Driven by greed, Saran set off to find the rock and eventually discovered it. Excitedly, he placed his shoulder against the rock and forced it back. Misery flew from the hole in a whirlwind of fury and clamped himself to Saran's shoulders. Saran howled in agony and tried to shake him loose, but Misery gripped him mercilessly. Saran pleaded to be released and tried to blame Yumart. In despair he screamed that he was innocent and that Misery had been trapped by his brother. But Misery just clung to Saran and snarled that he had been fooled once and would never be tricked again. Ahead of Saran lay the awful life that Yumart had suffered: his roubles would be wasted on unlimited vodka for Misery, who would now always be breathing down his neck.

Question box

Why was Saran rich?
Why was Yumart invited to the birthday celebration?
What did Misery force Yumart to sell?
How did Misery enjoy himself?
Why did Misery not believe Saran was innocent?

What events happened because Yumart was too generous?
What differences were there between Yumart and the other guests?
How do the first impressions of Misery suggest that he is not a cheerful person?
What made Saran search in the forest?
In what ways did Misery quickly show Saran that he was now going to lead an awful life?

Exploring ideas

1 See you next week

Saran is desperate to escape Misery. Imagine that he goes to his doctor to tell him the problem. Only Saran can see Misery, the doctor cannot.

The doctor begins to keep a weekly record of what Saran tells him on his visits.

Write the doctor's reports. Start each section with the heading: **WEEK ONE, WEEK TWO, WEEK THREE**, and so on.

Here is the first sentence to start you off for **WEEK ONE**:

> **WEEK ONE**. Today I was visited by an unhappy rich man who told me the wildest story . . . . .

2 The picture of misery

The only description of Mr Misery is of 'a gaunt figure . . . . . in the shadows'.

a) Write your description of Mr Misery. Pay attention to details of: face/voice/body/clothes/habits

b) Draw a picture to illustrate your idea of Mr Misery.

3 Oh brother!

Things that happen in childhood can give a good idea of what people will be like when they are older. Imagine that, when Saran and Numart were still young, their mother wrote to her sister, describing how very different her two boys were from each other. She did this by writing honestly about them and the things they had been doing.

Among other things, this letter told the boys' aunt:

a) how they were both treated.
b) how they got on with each other.
c) how they behaved with other people.

Write the letter. Begin:

>
>   Volga View,
>   Vroomsk,
>   Tartary
>   14th July
>
> Dear Nadya,
>   Thank you for your letter. I was glad to hear all your news. You ask about the boys . . . . .

4 Look at me

Everybody can spot a 'show-off'. Write about 'show-offs' you have known. Try and make clear if their behaviour was very irritating. Did they get away with it?

If you want to make it into an imaginary story, do so.

5 Helping hands

In any family it is important that people help each other.

Write from the point of view of each person in your family, including yourself, about what you think each does for the others. Some important things are easily taken for granted.

6 Excuse me for asking

People who save money can be seen as thrifty or miserly. Different types and ages do not always agree about saving money.

Be an interviewer, and find out what people think. A successful interviewer is always polite and interested.

Choose three people to interview:
a) somebody of about your own age
b) a parent, or other grown-up
c) a senior citizen

Here are some questions you could ask:

Question A How do you save money in any way?
Question B Has saving money ever been of real benefit to you?
Question C Do you think saving money can ever be a bad thing?
Question D Why is it a good idea for children to save money?
Question E Who would you ask if you were short of money?

Write up the interviews and add a conclusion of your own.

Discovering words

Learn the language

Here is an account of Saran's party as described by Yumart's wife:

'Saran was dressed *in bright, clashing colours* for his party, and he was celebrating *by showing off as much as possible*. Although we greeted him *with a great deal of respect*, he shouted at us *as though he wished us harm*. We stumbled into a dark corner of the room *feeling sorry for ourselves*. Many of the guests were dancing *in a noisy and high-spirited fashion*. Others were arguing *in an irritable way* or eating the food *with disgusting greed*. I was so proud of Yumart when he stood up *in such a determined manner* and his voice rang out *sounding sweet and tuneful*.'

Each of the groups of words in heavy italic type can be replaced by a single word. The ten words that will make sense are listed below:

boisterously	garishly	ostentatiously
deferentially	gluttonously	petulantly
disconsolately	melodiously	resolutely
vindictively		

Use your dictionary to discover what these words mean. Then rewrite the passage trying to choose the right word for the right place. These words which describe *how* things are done, are called **adverbs**. Look back to page 48 for more adverbs.

Make a stop

If something is a question, it has to be written with a final **question mark ?**

If something is said loudly, angrily or with astonishment, it needs an **exclamation mark !**

Here are some snatches of conversation that might have been heard at Saran's party:

1 Where is the birthday cake
2 Get out of my way
3 What a shock that was
4 Who is that man over there

5   Did you catch that superb fish yourself
6   You have just spilled sauce on my best dress
7   Whose party is this
8   Why on earth were those two invited
9   What a shame
10 Have you tasted that delicious jelly
11 Did you know you are sitting on my coat
12 I feel horribly sick
a) Rewrite these sentences, putting an exclamation mark or question mark as necessary at the end of each one.
b) Write *five* more things that Yumart could have heard at the party, that need either an exclamation or a question mark.

Try a new way

If you want to describe something in a sharp, colourful way, there is a whole set of lively phrases to help you. Although they can be puzzling if you try to understand them as *exact* descriptions, they do make sense if you let them *suggest* a feeling or a situation.

to laugh your head off
to keep your eyes peeled
to keep your nose to the grindstone
to get your teeth into something
to stick your neck out
to put your shoulder to the wheel

up to your eyes in it
to have an ear to the ground
to be led by the nose
to be down in the mouth
to stick in your throat

to twist someone's arm
to palm somebody off
to keep your hand in
to put your back into it

to get it off your chest
to use elbow-grease
to knuckle down
to be ham-fisted
to have no stomach for it

not to have a leg to stand on
to put your best foot forward

to be on your last legs
to keep on your toes

a) Find out the meaning of each of these phrases.
b) Put as many of them as you can into sentences about the people and events in the story of *The Two Brothers*.

Saran's unhappy birthday quiz-cake

Find the words from the story.

Across

1. to have Yumart under his control for a ___ (2 words)
2. Misery always became even more ___ and grumbled at Yumart
3. knowing that they could not avoid this ___
6. their poverty would contrast with his own worldly ___
7. Saran pleaded to be released and tried to ___ Yumart
8. laughing and singing with relief ___ be rid of his unwelcome guest
9. Ahead of Saran lay the awful life that Yumart had ___
12. ___ led Yumart into foolishness and waste.

Down

4. roubles, with which he could buy vodka when his hosts had been driven to ___
5. Sensing a chance to ___ Yumart flung himself desperately at the rock
9. In order to show how ___ he was
10. Driven by ___ Saran set off to find the rock
11. Yumart collected the bags of ___
13. Saran decided to visit him and learn his ___
14. In ___ he screamed that he was innocent
15. Saran howled in ___ and tried to shake him loose

The world of Yumart

This story is from Tartary, a region of Asia which has a proud history of its own, although it is now part of the Soviet Union. The fierce Tartar nomads needed tremendous determination when they defeated powerful enemies against overwhelming odds. Family loyalties were vital and, as the story shows, should never be ignored.

Who's in it?

Yumart..................a poor farmer
Saran....................his rich brother
Yumart's wife
Mr Misery
Merchants and their wives at a feast

What happens?

1. A poor farmer, Yumart, is hired by his rich brother, Saran.
2. Yumart and his wife are forced to attend Saran's birthday feast.
3. At this celebration, Yumart meets Mr Misery.
4. Misery stays with Yumart and brings him to the brink of ruin.
5. Yumart is made to carry Misery to his secret hoard in the forest.
6. When Misery gathers his rouble-bags, Yumart traps him under a rock.
7. Yumart, now rich, builds a good life for his family.
8. Saran visits Yumart to discover the source of his wealth.
9. Saran finds the rock in the forest and moves it.
10. Misery escapes, clings to Saran, and promises never to leave him.

Step into the drama world

Yumart suffers terrible misery, but it is his greedy brother who is the victim in the end.

Step one   He is ignored and humiliated.
Step two   He has to obey the orders of a hard master.
Step three   He succeeds in ridding himself of his unwanted visitor
Step four   His brother finally gets what he deserves.

And it *can* happen now . . . . .

Step one

Get into four groups

Each group sits in a circle. One person, sitting in the middle of the circle will try to get the others to answer or pay attention to him. Nobody may touch anyone else. The others will totally ignore this person. They will look at and talk to each other as though the one in the middle does not exist. The person in the middle scores a point if he manages to catch someone's attention. When the teacher calls 'Change', someone different sits in the middle. Who scores most points?

Step two

Find a partner

One person sits down, the other stands. The one sitting down is a robot, the other is the master. Every order that the master gives to the robot must be followed exactly. The robot will *never* do any more than it is instructed. The master can make the commands gradually more difficult, but *never* impossible.
The master must always be in complete control.
Change round.

Step three

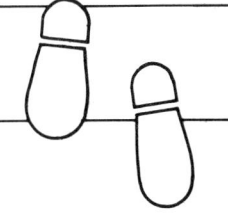

Groups of three: A, B and C

C came to stay with A and B for Christmas. It is now a month later and C is still there! A and B try to make tactful suggestions to persuade their visitor to go, but these do not work. So, in desperation, A and B plot to free themselves of C.
What happens?

Step four

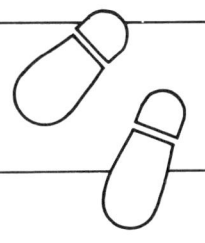

Groups of four or five

One of the group, X, is terribly mean.

Scene one: A situation arises in which X's meanness causes unhappiness and disappointment for the others.

Scene two: Not long after, something else happens. This time X's meanness leads *him* into real difficulties. The others are unable, or unwilling, to help him.

Act out both scenes.

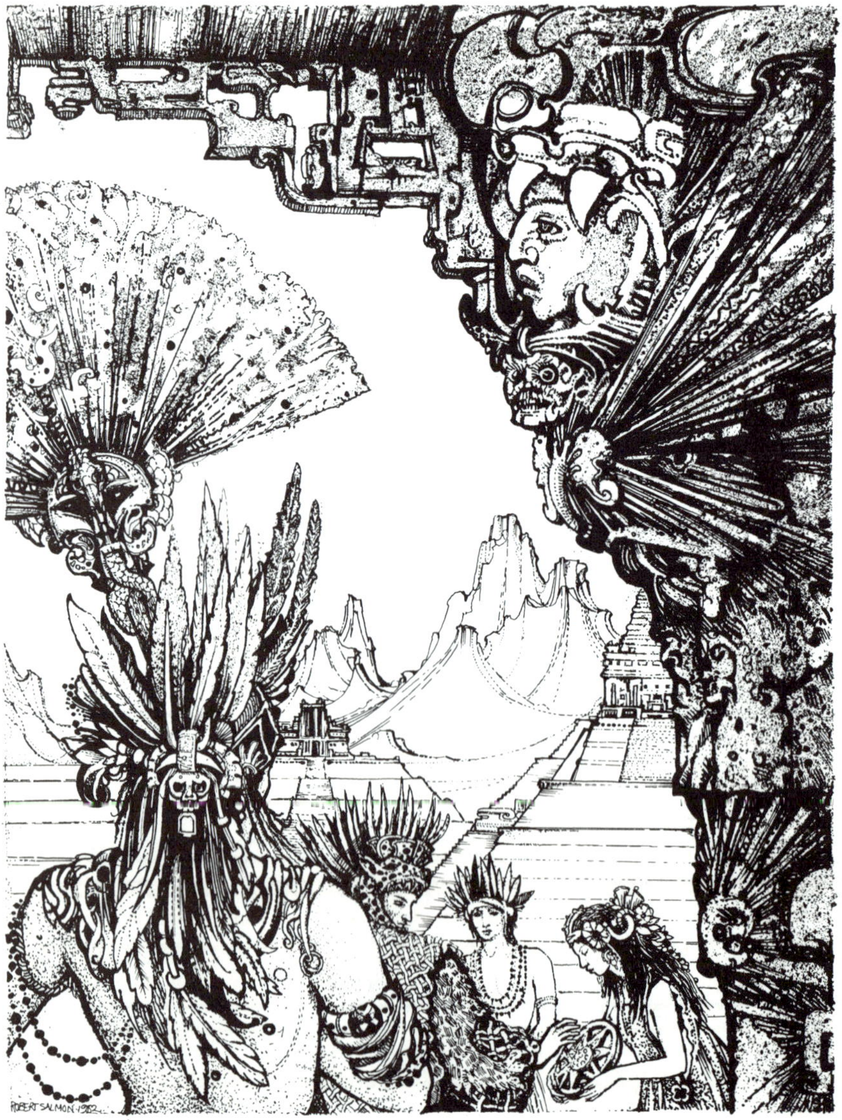
ROBERT SALMON · 1982

10 The world of wisdom

The Gift of the Gods

Poor and homeless, the tribes of the White Land had wandered for many years before they settled at the Moon Lake. There, on the islands and sandflats, they built a village of reeds which, in time, became the most marvellous city.

As the years passed and the number of people grew, there was no space for any more houses. The tribes began to fight each other until Quetzalcoatl, the feathered snake-god, instructed Tonalpoque, the high priest, to call the tribal leaders together.

These noble men mounted the temple steps, not knowing what awaited them. The wisest of them was Totochtin, whose family was both large and important. They all made offerings of incense and jade plates to show respect for the gods. When the high priest, wearing the robe of the jaguar, approached with his attendants, the leaders fell to their knees and listened.

Solemnly Tonalpoque told them that he had spent many hours studying the stone tablets that showed the count of days, and he had come to know the will of the gods. He had learnt that Quetzalcoatl wished one tribe to leave the city forever, taking with them only what they were able to bear on their backs.

As the leaders heard these words, they were all afraid that their tribe would be forced to leave the homes and possessions that they loved. Tonalpoque then announced that the gods had chosen Totochtin to serve them in this way. Totochtin rose heavily to his feet, bowed to the high priest, and agreed to obey the gods by leading his tribe from the city.

At this sign of consent, Tonalpoque took him into an inner chamber, thick with smouldering incense. The gods had guided the high priest to prepare gifts, one of which Totochtin could choose for the long journey ahead.

Two golden dishes were brought forward, covered in fine cloth. Tonalpoque revealed what lay beneath. On one there was the most perfect emerald Totochtin had ever seen; on the other were two short sticks of hard wood. A moment's thought was enough for the leader to make his choice. The high priest folded the cloth around the gift and placed it in Totochtin's hands.

Members of the tribe pressed round their leader when they saw him come from the temple. Already they had heard that they had been named by the gods to leave the city. They accepted this unwelcome decision, but were anxious to see what divine gift was to be theirs. As Totochtin unfolded the cloth and showed his people the two sticks of wood, they looked at him with undisguised disappointment, especially when they learnt that a perfect emerald had been offered to them. Some members of the tribe were close to tears; others were close to anger. It was difficult for them to hide their feelings and show obedience to their leader, but this they did.

Soon the people had to leave the city and travel for many days. When they had reached the mountains, they recognized how wise Totochtin had been. As they shivered in the cold, the tribe knew that an emerald, however perfect, would give them no comfort. But Totochtin took the temple-sticks, rubbed them together and produced the best gift the gods could provide, the warmth of fire.

One day the tribe would reach a new land in the mountains, where Quetzalcoatl had blessed the earth and made it rich. Here, with their sacred gift of fire, Totochtin and his people would live in peace and prosperity.

Question box

How was the first village built?
What did Quetzalcoatl look like?
What offerings were made to the gods?
Inside the temple, why did the leaders of the tribes become worried?
Where was the 'new land'?

Why did the tribes fight each other?
What was it like inside the temple?
How was the choice made as to which tribe should leave the city?
When did Totochtin's tribe show their loyalty?
How had Totochtin shown his wisdom?

Exploring ideas

1 ## The book of the new land

After their long journey, the tribe of Totochtin had to build a new city up in the mountains. All they had with them was what they had carried on their backs.

   How would they have chosen the place?
   How would they have begun to make their homes and feed themselves?
   What difficulties might they have faced?

Imagine that you are one of the tribe who has been appointed to write '*The Book of the New Land*'. It is many years since the tribe arrived in the New Land and a city has now been built. It is your task to write about everything that happened, giving all the details that future generations ought to know.

2 Jigsawruses

Quetzalcoatl was said to be a mixture of a snake and a bird. There are other creatures in myths and legends which are also strange combinations:
basilisk . . . centaur . . . chimera . . . gorgon . . . griffin . . . minotaur . . . satyr . . . siren . . . sphinx . . . unicorn

a) Find out what these creatures were supposed to look like.

b) Invent a 'mixed-up creature' of your own. Describe its appearance and how it lives. Give it a name and draw a picture of it.

3 Room to breathe

When the people of the White Land started to fight each other, it was because the city was too crowded. Think of the many problems there could be with too many people in too little space.

If you were the leader you could arrange an interview with Tonalpoque to put your tribe's point of view. You will need to describe the variety of unpleasant problems and how they are making your people miserable. Your speech should aim to persuade Tonalpoque that something *must* be done.

Write down what you would say.

4 Follow your leader

Not everyone wants to be a leader. Some people, however, make a good job of it. Sort out the 'qualities' from the list below that you consider a leader ought to have.

strong	generous	fond of animals	imaginative
good-looking	old	well-spoken	friendly
helpful to others	brave	good at sport	persuasive
well-dressed	bossy	big	bold
able to make decisions	rich	clever	sympathetic

Write down the things that you feel are important, and explain why each one could help to make a good leader.

What else would you expect from a leader?

5 Fire escape!

In the story, fire is a friend. It *can* be a foe.

a) Think of as many ways as you can in which fire could break out in your home.

b) If you were at home when a fire started, you might have to leave the house very quickly. Imagine you can take with you anything you can carry, but you have time to make only one journey.

Write the story of 'Fire Escape!'. Make clear what you choose to rescue and what dangers threaten you.

6 Just what I wanted

As a joke, you have sent an unusual present to an old friend. You have chosen it very carefully . . . . . . it is totally useless as far as you can see.

To your amazement you receive a serious and very grateful thank-you letter. This letter explains, in detail, the reasons why the present is so welcome. Your friend has seen uses for the gift which you find most surprising.

Write this unexpected thank-you letter.

Discovering words

Make a stop
Make a copy of the 'tablet' putting capital letters only where they are necessary: the names of particular people or places, the names of days and months, and the word 'I'. Every new sentence, of course, should also begin with a capital letter.

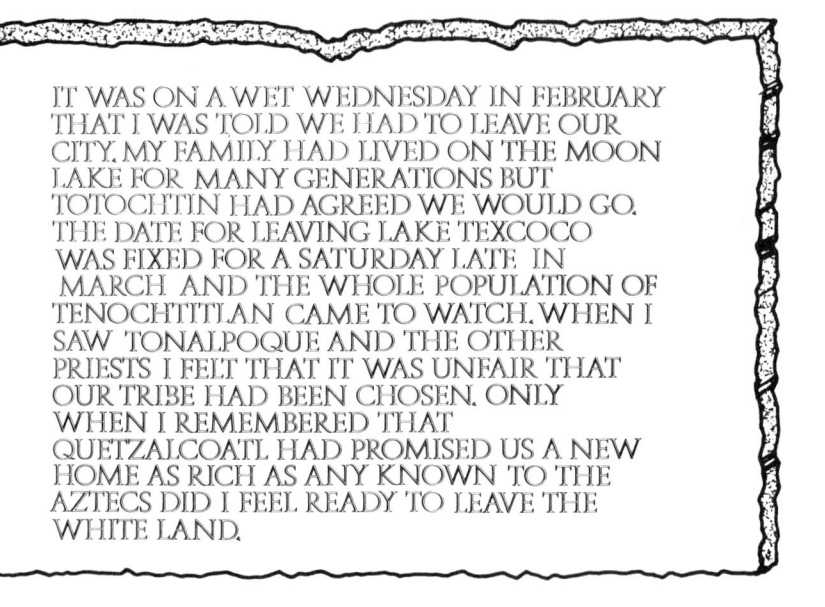

> IT WAS ON A WET WEDNESDAY IN FEBRUARY THAT I WAS TOLD WE HAD TO LEAVE OUR CITY. MY FAMILY HAD LIVED ON THE MOON LAKE FOR MANY GENERATIONS BUT TOTOCHTIN HAD AGREED WE WOULD GO. THE DATE FOR LEAVING LAKE TEXCOCO WAS FIXED FOR A SATURDAY LATE IN MARCH AND THE WHOLE POPULATION OF TENOCHTITLAN CAME TO WATCH. WHEN I SAW TONALPOQUE AND THE OTHER PRIESTS I FELT THAT IT WAS UNFAIR THAT OUR TRIBE HAD BEEN CHOSEN. ONLY WHEN I REMEMBERED THAT QUETZALCOATL HAD PROMISED US A NEW HOME AS RICH AS ANY KNOWN TO THE AZTECS DID I FEEL READY TO LEAVE THE WHITE LAND.

Watch your step
Decide which is the correct meaning of each of the following:

1. If you are *in hot water*, are you:
   a) excited   b) feverish   c) in trouble?

2. If you are talking *hot air*, are you:
   a) very angry   b) talking without knowledge
   c) discussing climates?

3. If you *add fuel to the fire*, are you:
   a) increasing someone's annoyance
   b) gathering dry wood   c) calming someone?

4. When you meet an *old flame*, have you come across:
   a) an idea of great value   b) a retired seaman
   c) a person you were once fond of?

5 If you *blow hot and cold*, are you:
   a) for something, and then against it
   b) stepping into a warm room   c) out of breath?
6 When you *play with fire*, do you:
   a) act stupidly   b) get upset   c) take risks?
7 If you get *hot under the collar*, are you:
   a) wearing a tight shirt   b) becoming annoyed
   c) having a brain wave?
8 If you *go through fire and water*, do you:
   a) lead a varied life   b) make an awkward journey
   c) overcome many difficulties?
9 When you *warm to an argument*, do you:
   a) become confused   b) start to enjoy a discussion
   c) think something is ridiculous?
10 When you do something *in the heat of the moment*, is it done:
   a) rashly   b) very skilfully   c) in summer-time?

Learn the language

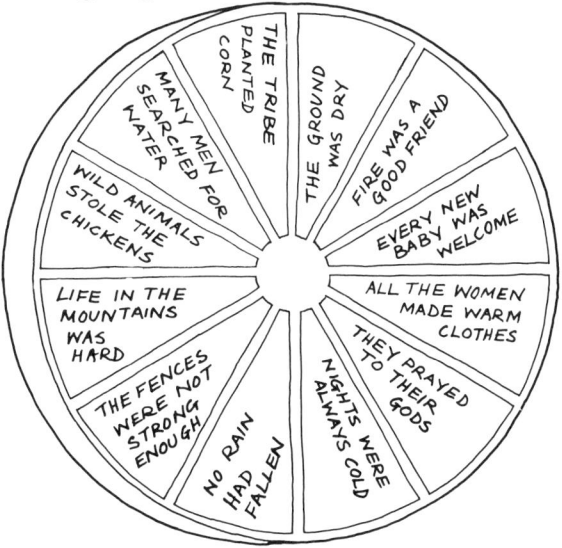

(Wheel diagram with segments:)
- THE TRIBE PLANTED CORN
- MANY MEN SEARCHED FOR WATER
- WILD ANIMALS STOLE THE CHICKENS
- LIFE IN THE MOUNTAINS WAS HARD
- THE FENCES WERE NOT STRONG ENOUGH
- NO RAIN HAD FALLEN
- NIGHTS WERE ALWAYS COLD
- THEY PRAYED TO THEIR GODS
- ALL THE WOMEN MADE WARM CLOTHES
- EVERY NEW BABY WAS WELCOME
- FIRE WAS A GOOD FRIEND
- THE GROUND WAS DRY

Linking-words are called **conjunctions**. For instance:

since   if   when   while   although   so   until   but   because   whenever   as   before

See how many new, different sentences you can make by joining sentences from the wheel together with conjunctions. All sentences must make sense.

The Aztec temple quizword

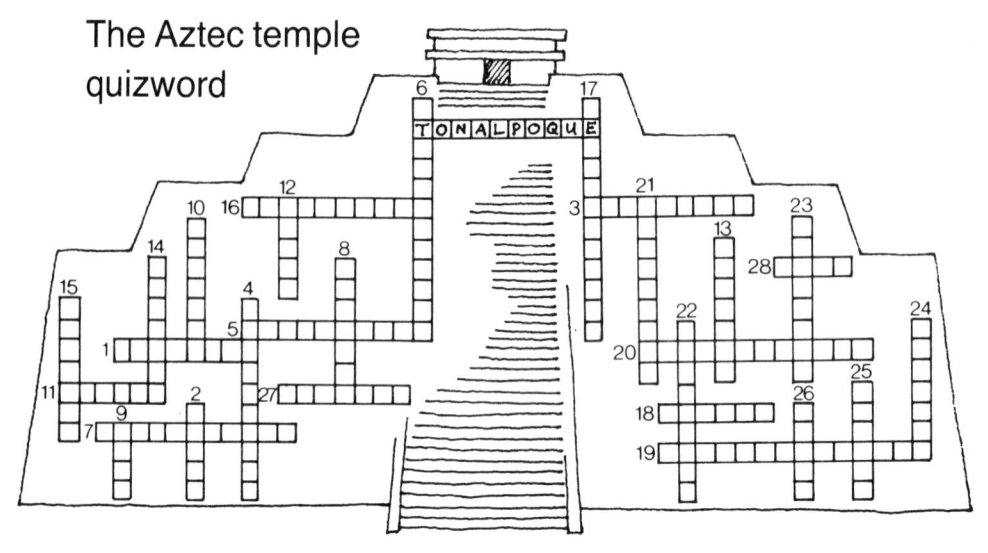

Find the words from the story.

1. Quetzalcoatl, the feathered ___-___ (2 words)
2. These ___ men mounted the temple steps
3. The wisest of them was ___
4. They all made offerings of incense and ___ (2 words)
5. When the high priest, wearing the robe of the jaguar, approached with his ___
6. he had spent many hours studying the ___ (2 words)
7. that showed the ___ (3 words)
8. As the ___ heard these words, they were all afraid
9. agreed to ___ the gods by leading his tribe from the city.
10. an inner chamber, thick with smouldering ___
11 & 12 The gods had ___ the high priest to prepare ___
13. Totochtin could choose for the long ___ ahead
14. there was the most perfect ___ Totochtin had ever seen
15. A moment's ___ was enough
16. The ___ folded the cloth around the gift (2 words)
17. they had been named by the gods to ___ (3 words)
18. showed his people the two ___ of wood
19. they looked at him with undisguised ___
20. Some members of the tribe were ___ (3 words)
21. It was difficult for them to hide their feelings and show ___ to their leader
22. When they had reached the ___
23. As they ___ in the cold
24. an emerald, however perfect, would give them no ___
25. the best gift the gods could provide the ___ of fire
26. One day the ___ would reach a new land
27. Quetzalcoatl had ___ the earth
28. their sacred gift of ___

122

The world of Totochtin

This story comes from the Aztecs who ruled a vast empire in South Mexico until the Spaniards conquered them in the sixteenth century. The Aztec capital of Tenochtitlan, built on islands in Lake Texcoco, was a marvellous example of their skill and ingenuity. Whatever the gods willed, the Aztecs believed that their instructions should be obeyed.

Who's in it?

Quetzalcoatl...(Kwet-zel-car-tel)..........the feathered snake-god
Tonalpoque...(Tonal-po-kway) ....the high priest
Totochtin...(Ter-tok-tin) ....leader of a tribe
Other leaders, members of tribes, attendants on the high priest.

What happens?

1. The people of the White Land build homes on islands in the Moon Lake.
2. The city becomes too crowded and fighting breaks out between the tribes.
3. The god, Quetzalcoatl, decides that one tribe must leave the city.
4. The leaders of the tribes are summoned by Tonalpoque, the high priest.
5. They are worried as to who will have to leave the city.
6. When his tribe is chosen, Totochtin accepts the decision.
7. He chooses two sticks, rather than a perfect emerald, to take on the journey.
8. His tribe is disappointed when they learn of the gift selected for them.
9. On the long journey, Totochtin uses the sticks to produce fire for vital warmth.
10. The tribe reaches a new land where they live in happiness.

Step into the drama world

Totochtin and his tribe are chosen to leave the crowded city to find a new home far away:

Step one   There are too many people in too small a space.

Step two   An unwelcome decision is accepted without complaint.

Step three   A less attractive gift turns out to be just what is needed.

Step four   Although they meet problems, everyone makes the best of things.

               And it *can* happen now . . . . .

Step one

Divide into two equal groups

Sit down in two large circles. Give each person a number. When the teacher calls a number, that person has to go and stand in the middle of their circle.

Other numbers are called, and the game is to get the whole group standing as close together as possible *without touching*.

Step two

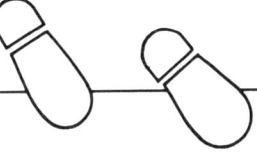

Find a partner, A and B

You are children in the same family. A has been told that he is to stay with a relative who lives some distance away in a rather dull town.
B is very pleased that he has not been 'chosen'. He tries to annoy A by hinting that the time ahead is likely to be unpleasant.
A, however, thinks of so many advantages that B begins to wish that he could go. He may even try to get A to change places with him.
Act it.

Step three

Groups of three or four

It is Christmas Day. Presents are being unwrapped with much excitement.
Everybody has received just what they wanted, except for one person who is disappointed with the present of *a small torch*.
As it grows dark, however, the gift of the torch turns out to be very useful more than once.
What happens?

Step four

Groups of four/five

You have gone camping together. When you arrive at the field where you wish to stay, you discover that you have left important things behind, for example: can-opener, tent-poles, matches, cutlery, cooking pots etc.
While everyone else is dismayed, one member of the group refuses to give up. Gradually this good humour encourages everyone to make the best of things. It may turn out to be better than anyone could have expected.
One of the group will give the final line:
        'This is going to be the best holiday ever!'

Answers

Chapter One: **Read the signs** (page 13)

The predictions are:
You will live in London. You have been elected to be a Member of Parliament in the House of Commons (Big Ben, River Thames.) You will serve for ten years. (Two periods of five years each.)
You will fall in love with a nurse or doctor and marry this person. You will have four children; two sets of twins. Each pair will be a boy and a girl.
You will fly to Japan and then on to America where you will live.

Chapter Four: **Read the signs** (page 49)

1. Travel huge distances at each stride
2. The ability to see into the future
3. London
4. Rome
5. Moon, Tiw, Wodin, Thor, Freya, Saturn, Sun (Tiw, Wodin, Thor and Freya were Norse gods)
6. North and South Atlantic, North and South Pacific, Arctic, Antarctic, Indian Ocean
7. St George of England, St Andrew of Scotland, St Patrick of Ireland, St David of Wales, St Denis of France, St James of Spain, St Antony of Italy
8. Pride, Covetousness, Lust, Envy, Gluttony, Anger, Sloth
9. 1756–1763 in western Europe
10. The Pyramids of Egypt, The Hanging Gardens of Babylon, The Temple of Diana at Ephesus, The Pharos lighthouse at Alexandria, The Statue of Zeus at Athens, The Colossus of Rhodes, The Mausoleum at Halicarnassus
11. Bashful, Doc, Dopey, Grumpy, Happy, Sleepy, Sneezy

Chapter Five: **Watch your step** (page 60)

1) = b 2) = a 3) = c 4) = c 5) = b 6) – b 7) – c 8) – b
9) = a 10) = b

Chapter Eight: **Read the signs** (page 97)

1 = an arrow 2 = a drum 3 = a river 4 = a forest 5 = reeds
6 = Love

Chapter Ten: **Watch your step** (page 120)

1 = c 2 = b 3 = a 4 = c 5 = a 6 = c 7 = b 8 = c 9 = b
10 = a

Index: Exploring ideas

This index gives an idea of the range and location of activities. (Several are awkward to categorize, and could appear under more than one heading.) The first number is the page, the second is the section.

	Page		Page		Page
Advertisement	83(6)	Fable	59(6)	Narratives	21(1)
		Interviews	81(2)		34(1)
Autobiography			107(6)		46(3)
	94(4)	Lateral	10(3)		83(5)
		thinking	35(6)		93(1)
Cautionary	22(3)		46(1)		117(1)
tales	47(6)		57(1)	Newspaper	11(5)
			70(2)	story	
Charts	22(4)		81(1)		
	58(3)			Obituary	69(1)
	94(2)	Legend	46(4)		
Curses	70(4)			Personal	23(6)
		Letters	47(5)	experiences	71(6)
Descriptions			106(3)		106(4)
	10(2)		119(6)		119(5)
	21(2)	Logical	23(5)		
	46(2)	thinking	34(2)	Poems	11(6)
	58(2)		59(4)	Priorities	9(1)
	71(5)		70(3)		95(6)
	82(4)	Magazine	95(5)		118(4)
	106(2)	column		Radio	59(5)
	118(2)			bulletin	
		Myths	10(3)		
Diary form	34(4)		35(5)	Speeches	82(3)
	105(1)				118(3)

Index: Discovering words

Page references

Adjectives 24/84
Adverbs 48/108
Alphabetical
  sequence 48
Apostrophes 84
Capital Letters
  12/120
Conjunctions 60/121
Dictionary
  work 13/60/108
Direct
  speech 72

Encyclopedia
  work 49
Exclamation
  marks 108
Full Stops 12
Idioms 109/120
Nouns 13/72
Plurals 72
Proverbs 96
Question
  marks 108

Riddles 97
Script writing 25
Similes 36
Slang 37
Title
  punctuation 61
Tongue
  twisters 73
Verbs 36/96
Word
  Confusion 24/85